# HANDBOOK OF
# LAGO ARGENTINO
# & GLACIAR
# PERITO MORENO

*Miguel Angel Alonso*

# HANDBOOK OF
# LAGO ARGENTINO
# &
# GLACIAR
# PERITO MORENO

*Miguel Angel Alonso*

**ZAGIER & URRUTY**
PUBLICATIONS

Although the author and publishers have exhaustively researched all sources to
ensure the accuracy and completeness of the information contained in this book, we
assume no responsibility for errors, inaccuracies, omissions or any inconsistency
herein. Any slights of people or organizations are unintentional.

First Edition in Spanish 1994, Zagier & Urruty Publications ISBN 1-879568-22-5
First Edition in English 1994, Zagier & Urruty Publications ISBN 1-879568-23-3
Fourth Edition in English 2004, Zagier & Urruty Publications ISBN 1-879568-23-3

Library of Congress Catalog Card Number: 96-61241

**ZAGIER & URRUTY**
P U B L I C A T I O N S
P.O. Box 94 Sucursal 19 — C1419ZAA Buenos Aires — Argentina
☎ (54-11) 4572-1050 — FAX (54-11) 4572-5766
info@zagier.com
www.patagoniashop.net

**PUBLISHERS OF**
Trekking in Chaltén & Lago del Desierto
Ecomap Parque Nacional los Glaciares
La Patagonia vieja
La Patagonia trágica
Trekking Map Patagonian South Icefield
Trekking Map Monte Fitz Roy / Cerro Torre / Lago del Desierto
**BOOKS, GUIDES AND MAPS CATALOG IN THE WEB**

*To Leslie*

# TABLE OF CONTENTS

**Los Glaciares National Park** .............................. 9

**Glaciers and Glaciations** ..................................... 11
Introduction • Glaciology beginnings • Glaciations causes
• Glaciations in Patagonia • Glaciations in our area •
What is a Glacier? A two act drama • Kinds of Glaciers
• The Patagonian Icefield • Ice in the World

**Perito Moreno Glacier** .......................................... 33
Biography of the Perito Moreno • Perito Moreno Glacier:
data and characteristics • A bit of History • The Breaking: The whims of a giant • Upsala Glacier

**Geology of the Region** .......................................... 47

**History** ................................................................. 51
American populating • The Tehuelches • The world
according to the Tehuelches • Explorers • The Settling
of Lago Argentino • Andreas Madsen, an austral pionner
• The beginnings of El Calafate • Climate • The
Patagonian wind

**Flora** .................................................................... 69
A botanic look throughout the zone

**Fauna** .................................................................. 81

**Patagonian Marine Fauna** ................................... 99

**Patagonian Estancias** ......................................... 115
History • Calendar of activities • El mate

**Two Mountains, Two Legends, Two Conquests** ........... 129
Lionnel Terray, Guido Magnone and the Conquest of
Fitz Roy • Cesare Maestri and the Torre Peak: A mith
of stone

**Bibliogaphy** ........................................................ 139

**Services, Tours & Trekking Guide** ...................... 141
Inns, restaurants, transportation, excursions and
walks in the National Park, El Calafate and El Chaltén

# INTRODUCTION

Every trip means getting close to other lands and other people, not only physically but spiritually as well.

I simply seek this through this book: to get you a little closer to this breathtaking region of glaciers, lakes and steppes.

I hope to make your trip more fruitful, and that you take a bit of Patagonia back with you in your luggage, for if when you are far away you should want to get close to it again.

M.A.

# Los Glaciares National Park

**Los Glaciares** National Park, within whose jurisdiction great part of the region described in this book is enclosed, was created in 1937, to preserve the natural wonders of this part of the Austral Patagonian Andes.

It covers 6000 km², of which one fourth belongs to the National Reserve and the other three specifically to the Park.

Its limits to the West always follow the Chilean-Argentine international dividing line between the parallels 49° 15' and 50° 50' South (from Mount Fitz-Roy to Mount Stokes) comprising part of the Southern Patagonian Icefield and all the glaciers that come down from it toward the East.

Partly due to its special landscape and partly to its flora and fauna in danger of extinction, in 1981, UNESCO declared the area a **Natural Patrimony of Humanity**.

Besides the Central Administration, located in Calafate, the Park has four sections (**Lago Roca, Río Mitre, Glaciar Perito Moreno and Chaltén**), permanently open, where visitors can obtain all information regarding the zone, fishing licenses, camping sites, etc.

For visitors own safety, as well as for the conservation of the Park, we request to follow the parkguards instructions at all times, and not to litter the landscape.

Finally, we would like to strongly recommend a visit to the **Chaltén** Region, at the northern end of the Park, where well demarcated trails, together with the spectacularity of the mountains (Fitz-Roy, Cerro Torre...), have made this a true Mecca in Patagonia for the trekking and mountain hiking lovers.

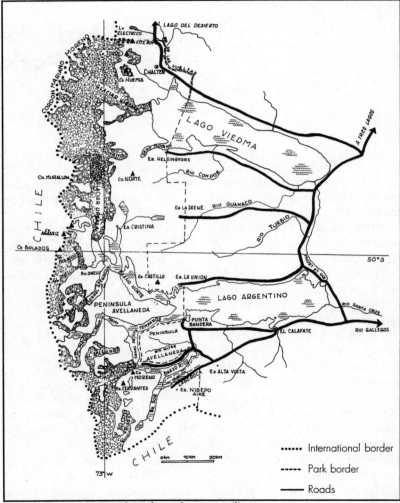

**Los Glaciares National Park and surroundings**

# Glaciers and Glaciations

## Introduction

About 18000 years ago, during the peak of the last glaciation, glaciers covered one third of the surfacing lands, which represented over three times their current extension. Sea level decreased 120 m, and so some of today's great extensions of land covered by sea water, were at that time solid ground. The latter, accounts for the human and animal migrations that marked that period. In those days it was possible to walk from Siberia to Alaska, thus the populating of America began; or from Europe to England, among other examples.

Due to the plastic texture of the magma underlying the crust of the earth, the land submitted to the pressure of ice sunk under the polar ice sheets, as it occurs at present in Antarctica and Greenland. Gradually, as the ice withdrew, the land slowly began to rise again. This phenomenon has not yet concluded. (It has been calculated, that even today, Greenland rises 1 m per century). The inhabitants of a small archipelago off the coast of Finland, have mostly benefitted from this fact. Every 50 years, for the last centuries, they have had the pleasant task of allocating the lands that the sea discloses.

As impressive as today's glaciers may seem, they are only a small reminder of the frozen extensions of the past. Nevertheless, today they still play a very important role: they occupy 10%

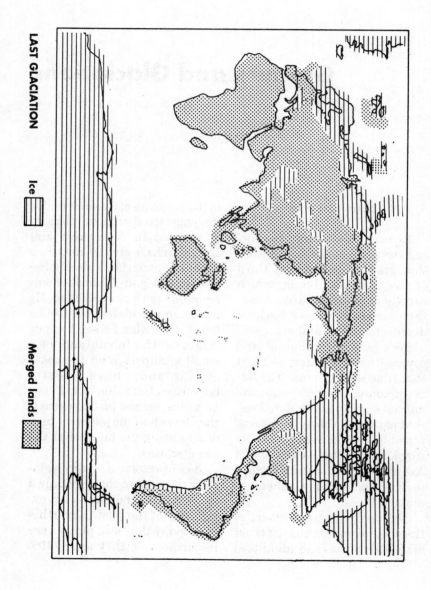

LAST GLACIATION

Ice

Merged lands

of the surfacing lands that represent 90% of the fresh water of the planet. (This is an important fact in a world where drinking water is becoming scarce and more contaminated). Moreover, the air draughts and water flows they produce, help to balance the earth's climate, which would be suffocating without them.

Glaciers were also responsible in the past, for the digging, conveying and pulverizing of all kinds of minerals which violent tempests blew all over the world creating very rich soils for agriculture.

During the peak of glaciation, the decrease in the mean temperature, greatly varied throughout the world: ten degrees less in Alaska, six in England, two in the Tropics and almost no change in the Equator.

Today's forecasts show, that if the glaciers should melt at present, the sea level would rise between 60 and 70 meters; huge extensions of coastal lands and

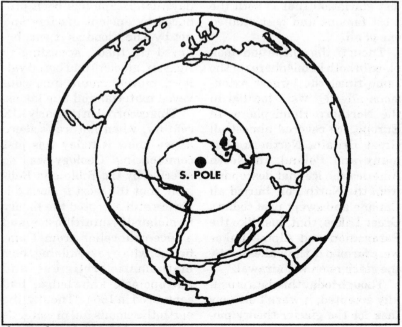

**The Earth 450 000 000 years ago**

some of the most important cities of the world would flood.

Though today we know that the glaciation phenomenon has repeatedly occurred since remote geological ages in different parts of the world (450 million years ago, before the continents separated, the Sahara Desert was precisely located at the South Pole and was undergoing an enormous glaciation. Even today, the grooves you find on the smooth rock surfaces, are visual evidence of this occurance). In this book, we will refer to the last glaciation that is both the most famous and best studied one of all.

Though the glaciation took place in both hemispheres at the same time, the largest extensions affected were located in the Northern Hemisphere. In Europe, ice covered almost all Great Britain, Northern Germany and Poland; in North America the ice that descended from the North Pole buried all Canada and swept past today's Great Lakes, that, just like the Patagonian and Alpine Lakes were formed in the wakes left by the glaciers on withdrawal.

Though today this data is usually accepted, it wasn't an easy task for the glacier theory pioneers to convince their contemporaries of the role the glaciers had played in the formation of the current landscape. Let's see how this all began:

## Glaciology Commences

In 1837, a Swiss scientist, Louis Agassiz, who till then had been admired for his knowledge on marine fossils, sets forward a theory that, in the opinion of his eminent colleagues within the scientific community, is considered no less than a blasphemy during a High Mass. "Today's landscape has been produced by ancient glaciers and not by The Flood as it was believed till then", according to Agassiz, glaciers had bored valleys, moved mountains, conveyed material and dug lakes.

This occurred in the early XIX century, when natural science as we know it today was just commencing. Geology was so affected by the Bible and Religion, that the most famous followers still accepted the theory formulated by an archbishop and a vice-chancellor from Cambridge, who by assembling their mathematic, religious and antropologic knowledge, had sentenced in 1654. "The sky, the earth, the clouds full of water as well as mankind were created

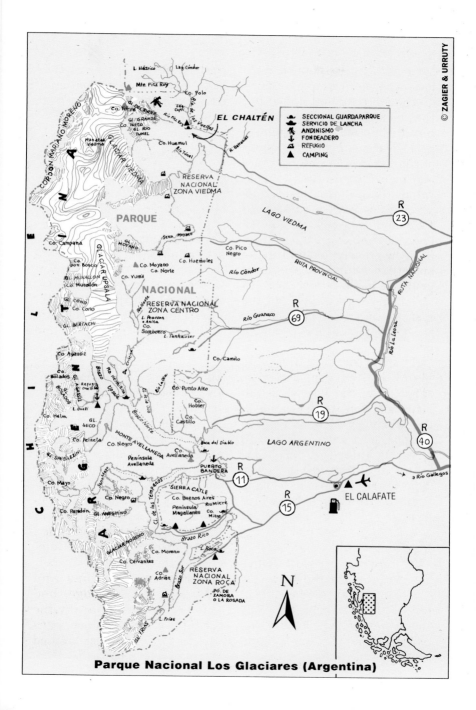

**Parque Nacional Los Glaciares (Argentina)**

Glaciar Perito Moreno - *Perito Moreno Glacier*

El Fitz Roy y el Torre vistos desde el Hielo Patagónico - *Fitz Roy and Cerro Torre as seen from the Patagonian Icefield*

Volcán Lautaro

by the Holy Trinity on October 26, 4004 B.C. at 9 AM."

It was a time when all that was inexplicable was always related to witchcraft; such was the case of the erratic blocks, those enormous rocks scattered all over the country in Northern Europe, which had no connection whatsoever with the surrounding landscape, and as Agassiz would later explain had been taken from their original locations to their current ones by the glaciers.

As the XIX century goes by, Agassiz theories, as well as their derivations, become more accepted: i.e. the decrease in sea level, the sinking of land under the weight of ice, the rising of that land after the ice thawed, the formation of moraines, the conveying of erratic blocks...

At the beginning, it was believed that there had only been one great glaciation. Later the findings of vegetable remains between the moraine layers aroused the idea that a better climate had taken over the areas covered by ice every time the ice had withdrawn, and thus had allowed the rebirth of life, till the ice would move forward again, covering everything once more: The idea of **Glaciations** had begun.

From then on, glaciology has been considered a tool to discover the earth's climate in remote times and in different places around the world. The setting forth and withdrawal of ice would be related to successive cooling offs and heating ups of the earth. This tool is still used today by scientists who study the polar ice sheets of Antarctica and Greenland trying to explain the earth's climate in the past.

The surveys carried out at the end of last century in North America and Europe, which were the locations of the great glaciations of the Pleistocene, revealed identical data for the great glaciations of this geological age, that approximately covers the last 2 million years.

Surveys also proved that the great ice invasions, were produced in both hemispheres at the same time and followed the same course.

### Glaciations Causes

The causes for all these climatic changes, still had to be solved: All kinds of theories had been considered till then; the rising and contraction of the crust of the earth; great volcanic eruptions that had launched such an amount of dust into the stratosphere as to reduce solar radiation, different activity in the solar spots...

Though all of them may be partially right, none thoroughly explains the phenomenon and even less its periodicity.

Today, the **Astronomical Theory** is the most accepted theory to explain the climatic variations that thus provoked the glaciations .

Already in the II Century BC, a Greek astronomer, Hiparco, discovered that the earth behaved as a top in space,; not only did it turn on itself, but its axis had a turning movement as well. Not knowing it yet, he had given the first step toward what later would be known as the astronomical theory of glaciations, that was thoroughly developed by the Yugoslavian mathematician Milutin Milankovitch, who devoted his whole life to elaborating very complex calculations, in his attempt to demonstrate that the interaction of 3 astronomical cycles altered solar radiations to the point of producing the cooling off of the earth that provoked the glaciations. The three cycles are:

1 - **Earth orbit cycle:** Every 100000 years the earth orbit around the sun, turns from an almost perfect circle into an almost perfect elipsis and later into a circle again.

2 - **Axial inclination cycle:** Every 41000 years, the earth's inclination on its orbit changes from 21.5° to 24.5° degrees and then back to 21.5°. This is the inclination that originates the seasons. The bigger the inclination, the more extreme the seasons (colder winters and warmer summers).

3 - **Precession of the equinoxes cycle:** Every 26000 years, like a top in space, the earth's axis describes a complete circle.

Curiously, it has been the seas, besides the geological observations, the ones that have definitely backed Milankovitch's astronomical theory. On analyzing and dating the sedimentation of the abyssal bottoms, it was possible to clearly determine the glacial cycles, due to the fact that the elements found could only exist in the presence of colder or warmer waters (microorganisms, different oxigen isotopes).

Anyway, the climatic mechanism is of such complexity, that even accepting the fact that the astronomical phenomenons were the principal causes for glaciation, it is also probable that other phenomenons, such as volcanic eruptions, solar spots, meteorites, etc. have participated, and still do in general climatic fluctuations. Regarding future forecasts on the climate based on surveys and past cycles, the matter becomes more complicated: the reckless use of the planet by the so called "homus civilizatus" is introducing new changes that widen the gap between the future and any scientific forecast, turning it more into a lottery game: the concentration of carbonic gas in the atmosphere due to the use of fossil fuel, the massive deforestation of the rainforests and an endless number of new ecologic alterations, that have been taking place during the last century, are factors never before encountered on Earth, and how to react to them arouses great controversy among scientists.

Regarding the massive deforestations, we must recall that there have been many theories that relate the massive deforestations that took place in Europe at the end of the Middle Ages, with the beginning of what was called "The Small Ice Age", when there was a general worsening of the climate that affected the Planet from XVI to XIX century.

## Glaciations in Patagonia

As impressive as our Patagonian glaciers or ice sheets may seem today, they are only small remainders of the great glaciations of the past. In Austral Patagonia, the first glaciation that left evident traces, occurred 3,5 million years ago, and the ice extended at least 60 km to the east of today's Andes Cordillera. Another great glaciation, which supposedly was the most important one that took place in Patagonia, occurred approximately 1 million years ago. The terminal moraines of the latter, can be seen in the southern plateau of the Santa Cruz River, at the height of Condor Cliff almost 200 km from today's Andes Cordillera.

Though there are some discrepancies on this point, today it is generally accepted that the ice only covered the most southern part of the Patagonian plateau, that is, to the south of Río Gallegos, where an enormous tongue extended over the Magellan Strait, (which is only another valley formed by ice and later invaded by the sea) and nearly all Tierra del Fuego, which is proved by the moraines that have been found under the current Atlantic sea level . In the rest of Patagonia, ice spread along great west-east axes (see map attached), and they never reached today's Atlantic coast.

During the geological period known as the Plestocene, that covers approximately the last two million years, glaciers ex-tended up to over 100 km be-yond the current east boundary of Lake Argentino, and in the Cordillera area, they surpassed 1,000 m above the current lake level. The decrease in sea level, located the Atlantic coast, 150 km to the east of the one we know today.

During warmer periods, that alternated with the glacial peri-ods, gigantic rivers produced by

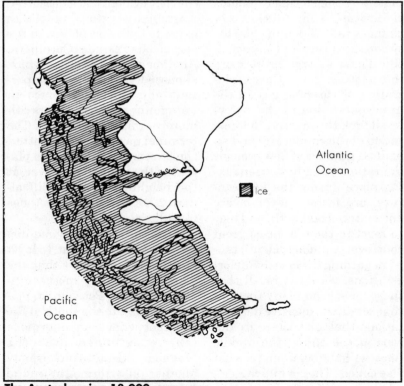

**The Austral region 18 000 years ago**

melt water, cut the plateaus toward the Atlantic, digging valleys along their way. Later on, during the subsequent glaciations, glaciers flowed through these valleys, both leaving material and burrowing the ground, with their enormous abrasive power, along their way. After the last withdrawal, the land revealed enormous basins that later filled with meltwater, thus forming the lakes that we know at present.

It is easy to understand why Louis Agassiz, the founder of the Glaciology, called the glaciers "God's Plows".

## Glaciations in Our Area

The following, is a short summary of the development of the stages of the last glaciation in Lake Argentino and Santa Cruz River.

• 18 to 20,000 years ago, during the maximum peak of the last glaciation, the glacial tongue that originated in the Cordillera, extended along today's Lake Argentino and Santa Cruz River up to the current location of Condor Cliff, 100 km to the East of the current eastern lake boundary.

• Later on, glaciers withdrew up to approximately their current locations.

• Then, a new ice spread occurred leaving us two series of moraines: the first one 25 km to the east of today's lake and later, the other one, that currently surrounds the lake near **Calafate** up to Cerro Frias. The latter is easily observed when traveling along the Calafate-Chalten Road; the permanent ups and downs in the road along 15/20 km after the paved road, indicate we are precisely on a moraine. One kilometer after crossing the Santa Cruz River, an enormous erratic block can also be seen at the side of the road.

• A new withdrawal toward the Cordillera; this is where the present Argentino Lake would be definitely formed. During this withdrawal (or maybe afterwards during a little new spread), both the moraines near Punta Bandera and the ones that surround the east part of Brazo Rico, which are easily seen from the road to Perito Moreno, were formed.

• Once the glaciers had withdrawn, to approximately their current locations, there was still in recent times, another ice spread, which has left terminal moraines between 2 to 10 km from the current glacier fronts.

We are referring to what was called "The Small Ice Age", that was a cooling off period that lasted from the end of the Middle Ages to the middle of the XIX century.

• From then on, and except in a few situations, the Patagonian glaciers, as the rest of the glaciers of the world as well, are withdrawing to a greater or smaller extent.

## What is a Glacier?
## A Two Act Drama

A glacier is usually compared with a river of ice. Though in certain aspects this is true, (they consist of a main stream and tributaries, they have erosive power, the flow speed is faster in the middle of the stream than on the margins) the latest studies reveal that the moving ice, which like all bodies react to gravity laws, also reacts to very specific behaviors that have nothing in common with water.

### Act 1: Formation

Glacier ice is but the product of snow compression under its own weight. Therefore, to form a glacier we need to fulfill a basic condition: That the snow fallen during a year in a certain area, be greater than the ablated

snow. So we can infer, that to form a glacier, we need not only great snowfalls, but even more important, to have an average annual temperature that allow to preserve the fallen snow. That is why the most important great ice extensions at present,–Antarctica, Greenland– are not located in the high Cordilleras at mean latitudes, –where, though snow fall is abundant so is summer fusion–, but at the extremes of each hemisphere where the scarce solar radiation does not allow the snow to melt. A typical example is found in Antarctica, which is considered a desert due to the snowfall, (between 120 and 140 mm annually in its central area) and that nevertheless, represents the most important ice concentration on the planet (90%), with ice thickness that sometimes surpasses 4500 m.

But let's return to the scenario of our first act: The fallen snow begins to compact as soon as it touches ground: the snowflakes, that are small granules of only one fourth mm thickness, of very original shapes, gradually change shape and begin to melt when coming into mutual contact, air is liberated from the intergranular spaces and clusters of them are converted into spherical grains. As new layers of fallen snow begin to accumulate, their weight continues to liberate air bubbles among the granules thus achieving more compactness, this process continues till ice is formed.

The time needed to form ice from snow, varies greatly from one glacier to another (from ten years, in temperate glaciers such as the Patagonian or Alpine glaciers, to several hundreds of years in Antarctica), depending on two factors: snowfall and temperature. Contrarily to what one might think, ice is more rapidly formed when glaciers are located in temperate climates. When we spoke about the melting granules, at temperatures over 0° C, this fusion become meltwater that percolates downward, then it refreezes and liberates small amounts of heat. This heat weakens the solidity of the lower granules that melt and then compact, hence allowing the faster formation of ice.

### Act 2.: Movement

A glacier is not only an ice

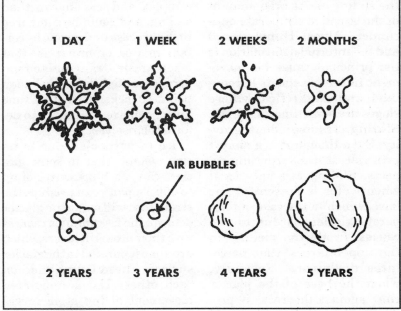

**From snow to ice**

mass, but most of all, an ice mass **in movement**. Obviously, as all bodies in movement along a slope, ice is affected by gravity and it is even more affected when the slope is steeper. This similarity with water is what has taken to compare glaciers with rivers for a long time, which though not completely false, after the latest surveys, is not completely true either.

According to glaciologists, a glacier carries out two kinds of processes: a sliding one and one of internal deformation. Both kinds appear in all glaciers, but the sliding one is predominent in the so called temperate ones (Andes, Alpes, Himalayas...) and the internal deformation is the principal cause for movement in the ice sheets (Greenland and Antarctica) where slopes are sometimes minimal. **Sliding**, of course is due to gravity. Even though it is a simple principle, it has surprising aspects. Sliding can only exist when water is present at the base, which in the case of temperate glaciers is due to two causes: firstly the melting in the upper layers, that percolates downward. Secondly, when the base of the glacier rubs against the rock, it produces a certain heat that also helps in the melting of small amounts of water.

Hence, a fine liquid film constantly runs along the base of the glacier working as a lubricant between the ice and the rock. This internal lubrication is one of the factors that determines the velocity of the glacier.

In the cold glaciers, the extreme temperature impairs any melting and the glacier becomes "welded" by its base: therefore the **internal deformation** of the ice will be the principal cause for its movement.

Internal deformation is more complex and less known than sliding, and could be compared to the process undergone by certain metals or minerals, that when under strain due to temperatures slightly below fusion point, as locksmiths of all time know, achieve the ability to deform themselves.

Ice in particular, due to its own weight, that in some glaciers can reach pressures of up to 650 Tn p/m$^2$, can produce the strain that will make the glacier deform: the ice granules reorganize their atoms in layers which are almost parallel to the glacier surface. These layers slide on each other. The accumulated movement of the atom layers within each granule, plus a certain skating effect between the granules, is what is called internal deformation. Paradoxically, the physical laws that rule this phenomenon are more similar to the flexion of red hot iron than to water flow along a duct.

But let's go back to the beginning of the act: we had said that a glacier is only a glacier if it moves. To start moving, ice needs to have a certain critical thickness of about 20 meters. From there on, three factors will de-termine the velocity of move-ment of the glacier: thickness, steepness and ice temperature. A greater thickness will make a glacier move faster, and obvi-ously a greater steepness of the slope it runs along, will produce the same effect.

We had spoke about cold and temperate glaciers: The more "temperate" the glacier, the faster it will be, due to the larger amount of meltwater that flows along its base and thus allowing

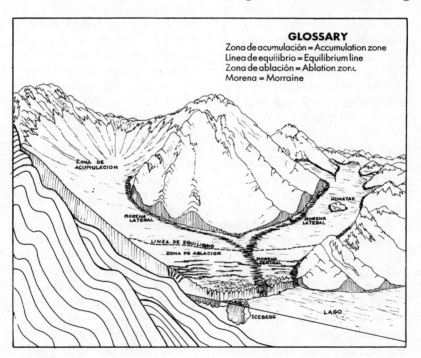

**GLOSSARY**
Zona de acumulación = Accumulation zone
Línea de equilibrio = Equilibrium line
Zona de ablación = Ablation zone
Morena = Morraine

its sliding, and due to the caloric energy liberated by some of the filtered water when refreezing, which helps weaken the ice granules making them more shapeable and easier to deform.

This same amount of meltwater running along the base and lubricating the ice friction against the rock, is the cause for a greater glacier velocity on hot or rainy days than on cold or dry ones, and logically also more in summer than in winter.

Hence, velocity, is a phenomenon that varies greatly according to the glacier and even in the same glacier. It does not only depend on the time of year, but also on the location: just like the water courses, the friction of its sides along the land, slows down the movement making it faster in the middle than on the sides. At the same time, basal friction, accounts for surface velocity being greater than the basal one.

A glacier's greatest velocity is found along its **equilibrium line**. This imaginary line divides a glacier into an **accumulation zone**, where annual snowfall surpasses the loss produced by evaporation or melting, and which coincides with the higher zones; and an **ablation zone**, where inversely to the latter, the snow loss is greater than the snowfall and evidently this corresponds to the lower zones of a glacier.

It is very important to delimit this line when studying a glacier, because both its location as well as the relationship between the two zones, are very important data to determine the glacier's behavior and its response to climatic changes. We could simply define this equilibrium line, as the series of points where there is still snow at the end of autumn, before the first snowfalls. It is more easily visualized in glaciers with many crevasses, because it draws the border between the crevasse zone and the zone where (at least the smaller ones) they are hidden under the snow. Logically, this line of permanent snow will change from year to year and from one glacier to another, and it depends on the orientation, slope conditions, etc.

**Moraines** are another common phenomenon to all glaciers and of a great help to scientists, we could briefly define them as an accumulation of stones, sand and clay carried by glaciers. Through them, we can learn the former positions of the glaciers. Moreover, from the study of organic remains among them, that can be easily dated using the Carbon 14 system, we can also learn the chronology of the past glacier movements.

According to their location, moraines can be classified into **lateral** or **central**. The latter, are produced when the lateral moraines of a glacier and its tributary meet, thus producing a characteristic stone line that runs along the center of a glacier, the same way it flows.

Another very important moraine for glaciologists, is the **terminus** moraine, that indicates the most extreme position reached by the ice and the spot where it began to withdraw.

To finish this brief introduction to glaciers, we would like to refer to **crevasses** and **seracs**, these are two very common aspects in all glacial geography, and they represent the greatest danger for those who walk on them. As we have already mentioned, the velocity of a glacier is not the same at all its points. Different velocities at different points, produce a stress on the ice plasticity that is not always completely absorbed and which will crack the surface (the crevasses are usually not deeper than 30 m). Due to the great pressure, the bottom is always compact. The **crevasses**, may greatly vary in length and depth, and they become specially dangerous for climbers when fresh fallen snow conceals them by forming bridges over them, but that at the same time are not solid enough to bear a person's weight.

When a glacier bed, has a very steep slope, its velocity may triple for some meters. This sudden change in speed, produces a series of cracked and very steep crevices, that form a chaotic accumulation of blocks or **seracs** that produce a very unstable balance. Any alteration caused by wind erosion, rain, temperature or a slight push from the ice that falls from above, may cause a landslide, that is the most common cause for mortal mountain accidents.

## Kinds of Glaciers

We can usually classify glaciers according to two factors: temperature and morphology.
• Regarding temperature, glaciers are divided into **cold** and **temperate** glaciers. The two great polar ice sheets (Antarctica and Greenland) correspond to the first kind, and all the rest are included in the second kind, i.e. the glaciers located in more

temperate latitudes.

• Regarding their morphology, we will mention some of the most common:

**Indlansis** or enormous horizontal ice sheets. Antarctica and Greenland are also the largest Indlansis, though other smaller ice sheets like the Patagonian Continental Ice and the ones of Iceland or the Spitzberg Islands could also be included.

**Cirque Glacier:** thus called because they occupy the higher parts of the mountain cirques.

**Valley Glacier:** the ones that run along a well defined valley.

**Piedmont Glacier:** they are valley glaciers, that occupy broad lowlands at the bases of mountain slopes, taking the shape of a fan.

**Compound Glacier:** it is a glacier that is nourished by smaller ones, as the tributaries of a river, they form a single course. The lateral moraines of the tributaries, become the central moraine in the principal glacier. In our region, an example of this kind is the Upsala Glacier.

**Calving Glacier:** the front of these glaciers is in contact with water, either lake or ocean water. In Lake Argentino there are three of the kind: Upsala, Moreno and Spegazzini and in Lake Viedma, the Viedma Glacier.

## The Patagonian Icefield

What are 17,000 km$^2$ of ice, a surface almost as big as Israel doing at a latitude that located in the Northern Hemisphere, would situate us in places like London, Paris or the USA-Canadian border, that are not exactly famous for their glaciers?

Surely anybody who has taken the time to closely look at a planisphere, has wondered about the subject. In the Northern Hemisphere, to find considerably large ice masses, you must go as far north as 60° (Iceland, South end of Greenland...). Instead in our hemisphere, the Patagonian Icefield extends from 47° to 51°, holding the record of having the closest glacier to the Equator, that reaches sea level. (San Rafael Glacier, Chile, 46° 45', this latitude corresponds to French Britain in Europe or Quebec in Canada). This cannot be explained by the height of the Cordillera, for in this area, the Andes mean altitude decreases in relation to more northern regions.

As Bob Dylan's song goes "The Answer is blowing in the Wind"

Who hasn't been shaken upon reading a novel on seafaring journeys of the navigators of the past? Discoverers, pirates, businessmen or adventurers, all who traveled these waters have told us tales about the "roaring forties", those hurricane winds that left so many shipwrecks along the Austral coast.

These winds, are the ones that blow between 40° and 50° degree south. They constantly blow Eastward. After traveling over the Pacific Ocean, they reach the Patagonian Andes, the only obstacle they find in their journey through the Southern Hemisphere, (Australia is 40° and New Zealand 45° =latitude), loaded with humidity.

When the winds encounter the Cordillera, the damp air begins to rise and get chilled, condensing itself at first into rain (the Patagonian Chilean Archipelagos are among the regions in the world with the greatest rainfalls, up to 4000 mm and 323 days of rainfall per year), later as it continues to rise and cool off, it turns into snow. The snowfall in this zone, reaches 5000 mm yearly, thus creating the conditions for the formation of an ice mass, that later flows along the various glacier streams, reaching, to the West, sea level in the Chilean Fiords, and to the East, the Argentine Lakes.

From the first expeditions that reached the **Ice**, at the beginnig of the century, both for its magnifecent geography, as well as for the sports challenge its difficult pathways and monstruous weather conditions represent, have made of the **Patagonian Icefield**, as the Chilean historian Mateo Martinic said " The last interior frontere of the American South in this century".

The following, is a transcription of a narrative passage of Dr. Reichert, the first man to reach the continental ocean water dividing line, in 1914, in a real sports prowess for the time: "We are at an extraordinarily savage place. A view that resembles Dante's Inferno opens into the valley of fiord and the traveler is shaken by the aspect of this world of eternal ice. An endless number of powerful and fantastic mountains, rise from a frozen sea that floods all the Cordillera. The glaciers, like frozen cascades run toward both sides of the slopes, they are the chaos of the entrails that feed the heart of the Cordillera and

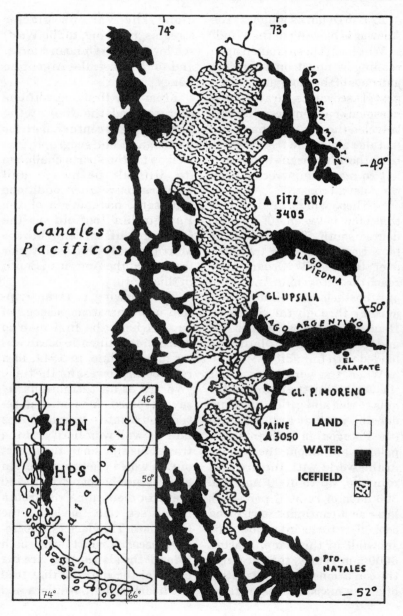

they give the landscape its great, desolated and cruelly wild character."

A mythical smoking volcano, that so many indian leyends, explorers and navigators of the last century and people of the zone spoke of, arouse great curiosity. Finally in January 1960, it was an Englishman, Eric Shipton who would discover a mountain in the midst of the Ice, "from where a dense vapor column rose several feet into the air"

There it was as last, the legendary volcano: it was Cerro Lautaro, one of the highest mountains of the **Patagonian Ice**, 3380 m.a.s.l., located at approximatelly 40 km NW of Fitz-Roy, which, had been wrongly taken for a volcano for a long time, as well.

**The Patagonian Icefield** is subdivided into two parts: **The North Patagonian Icefield** occupying 4200 km², totally located within the XI Chilean Region or Aisen. Mount San Valentin, 4060 m.a.s.l., is the highest peak in the Patagonian Andes and is in this part; and the **South Patagonian Icefield** occupying 13000 km² and which is shared between Chile and Argentina. It is 360 km long and 40 km (average) wide, though at some spots it reaches 90 km.

The **Patagonian Icefield**, is technically considered in glaciology, an ice mass of the "Indlansis" kind, a Norwegian word that means "ice among the mountains" because that is precisely what they are, ice caps that, at an average height of 1500 m.a.s.l. cover valleys between the mountain chains, and whose tops rise above the frozen plains. These immense frozen surfaces, are a vast zone of nourishment for the glacier tongues that flow both eastward and westward, the latter reaching the fiords and the Pacific channels. The most famous ones, because of their beauty and accesibility, are **Moreno** and **Upsala** in Argentina and **San Rafael** glacier in Chile.

At times, in the glacial plateaus, rock islands rise among the ice, these are known as "nunataks" an Esquimal word, and that are simply small mountains almost all covered by ice, whose very tops are only visible.

### Ice in the World

As to end this chapter I would like to give some brief data on the distribution of ice on the planet:

| | THOUSANDS OF KM² | % |
|---|---|---|
| ANTARCTICA | 12588 | 84.5 |
| GREENLAND | 1802 | 12 |
| ICELAND | 12 | 0.08 |
| EUROPE | 123 | 0.83 |
| CANADA | 178 | 1.20 |
| ASIA | 115 | 0.77 |
| ALASKA | 51 | 0.34 |
| SOUTH AMERICA | 26.5 | 0.18 |
| USA (Without Alaska) | 0.5 | 0.003 |
| OTHERS | 0.1 | 0.0007 |
| **TOTAL** | **14896.1** | **100** |

**Ice distribution around the world**

This data corresponds to the Flint Division in 1971.

We can infer from this data, that almost 97% of the planet's ice is concentrated in **Antarctica** and **Greenland** and which represents 98% of the fresh water reserves. In **Europe**, though the most famous glaciers are, of course, in the Alps, the vastest glacial areas are the Islands **Spitzberg** (Norway) and **Francisco José** (Russia).

Most of the **Asian** glaciers are in the **Himalayas**.

Regarding Africa, there are only a few small glaciers at the top of their highest mountains (**Kilimanjaro, Kenia, Ruwenzori**).

All the Southamerican glaciers are located on the Andes Cordillera from Venezuela to Tierra del Fuego, though the three quarter parts of the ice surface is concentrated in the **Patagonian Icefields**.

In **North America**, the largest ice concentrations are located in the **Noreast** islands of **Canada** and **Alaska**.

In **Oceania** most of the Glaciers are concentrated in the South Island of New Zealand.

Farolillo Chino - *Mizodendrum punctulatum*

Notro - *Embothrium coccineum*

Pan de Indio - *Cyttaria darwinii*

Zapatito de la Virgen - *Calceolaria biflora*

Topa-Topa - *Calceolaria uniflora*

Calafate - *Berberis buxifolia*

Arvejilla - *Lathyrus magellanicus*

Mata Guanaco - *Anartrophilum rigidum*

These are glaciers that due to their latitude, climatic conditions and origin, are very similar to the ones in **Patagonia**.

There are no glaciers in **Australia**.

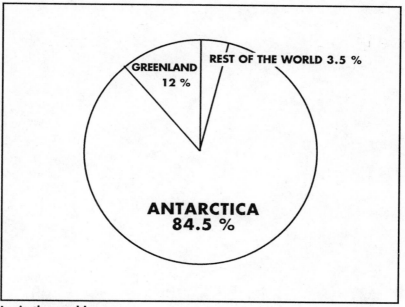

Ice in the world

# Perito Moreno Glacier

*To look at it, is to always see  it for the first time...*
*(J. L. Borges: The Sea)*

## Biography of the "Perito Moreno"

Though Moreno was not able to see the Glacier that was named after him, he deserves that honor for the explorations he carried out through these lands. As a tribute, we would like to give a short review on his life and work:

Francisco Pascasio Moreno was born in 1852, and from a very young age he developed a liking for Natural Sciences, to the point of organizing with his brothers and sisters, a private museum in the house attic. During his incursions in the country, together with the farm workers, he found a bone of an unknown animal that would later be named "Dasypus morenii" in his honor.

Encouraged by his readings on travels, at the age of 21 he travels to Carmen de Patagones, that was an authentic frontier in those days, and has his first contact with the indians.

The first problems of sovereignty with Chile in Austral Patagonia had begun. (Let's recall that Chile had made its first settlement in the Magellan Strait in 1849, that would later become today's city of Punta Arenas). In 1876, the Argentine government decides to send an expedition to investigate the Chilean whereabouts, because there is a rumor in Buenos Aires, that the neighbor country is trying to settle a colony at the mouth of the Santa Cruz River. Moreno embarks on this expedition, where he first takes contact with the principal problems he will devote his life to: exploring and appraising Patagonia, the limits with Chile and Argentine sovereignty.

A year later, now as a member of the board of directors of the Argentine Scientific Society, he organizes the first great expedition from Carmen de Patagones —on the Atlantic— to Nahuel Huapi Lake in the Cordillera. He crosses unknown indian territory at the time, and after an endless number of incidents he returns to Buenos Aires, where after writing the valuable reports on his journey, he immediately begins to prepare the next expedition: Now he decides to reach the source of the Santa Cruz River, following Fitz-Roy and Darwin's steps, and study the Cordillera in this area, because the situation with Chile was getting more tense.

They started out in October 1876, at the beginning of the next January, we find them going up the river, studying it inch by inch, in a small row boat that is towed from shore. After a month's effort, pursued by pumas and hunting guanacos and ostriches along the way, on January 13, 1877, they at last arrive at the lake he names "Argentino". They travel along its southern shore up to the Cordillera, both on foot and

on horseback, for the terrible tempests made navigation impossible in the precarious small boat. To the North, and going up La Leona River, (the name of Leona is due to a female puma (Felis concolor, American Lion, Cougar) which attacked him and nearly kills him), they arrive at Viedma Lake and still farther North to another lake, which he names after the Argentine Liberator, San Martin. Once they have fulfilled their reconnoitering mission, they return to Argentino Lake and go down again the Santa Cruz river. The 30 exhausting days it took them to go up the River, are only three days to go down, though the dangerous rapids they encounter on their way (it was March, and the river was at its maximum swell), almost put an end to the expedition, that was nearly over. On arriving at Pavon Island, at the mouth of the river, they continue on horseback to Punta Arenas, and from where they sail to Buenos Aires.

All the enormous amount of information and archeologic findings (fossils, stone instruments, and even a mummy he dug up close to where today's Calafate is), increase his private collection, that he would later offer for the founding of the

National Museum (today's Natural Science Museum in La Plata), of which he would remain perpetual director. He was then only 25 years old at the time.

Very soon, he leaves for the South again, on what would be his most unfortunate expedition: his purpose was to survey the Cordillera between today's towns of Esquel and Bariloche. He is captured by the Indians, close to Nahuel Huapi Lake, and after a thousand misfortunes where he almost losses his life, he is able to escape on a raft down the Limay River, until he is rescued, hungry and exhausted, 300 km downward.

Again in Buenos Aires, the crowds come to greet him. But the Government burocrats are not so happy. They recriminate him for not having followed the innitial plans for the expedition. Neither do they share Moreno's idea of an exhaustive study of the border to be able to better protect it. The point is, that tired and disappointed, Moreno resigns and leaves for Europe where he continues to develop his vocation for study and science. In 1884, we find Moreno again, organizing the Natural Science Museum in La Plata, to which he entirely devotes himself until 1896.

## The Argentine/Chilean Border Problem

In 1881, an agreement to determine the border lines between the two countries, was achieved with Chile. The text read: " The highest peaks that divided waters". It was very simple theoretically speaking, but not practically, because the line of the highest peaks, does not concide in many points with the line dividing ocean waters. Evidently, at each conflictive point, each country interpreted the Treaty in its favor, and in 1896 the two countries decide to end the divergency by an arbitrage of the English Government. Thus, a great activity begins by the Comissions appointed by each Government, each one commanded by an Expert (Perito) –that is why he went down in history as such–. There is a great difference between the two experts: while the Chilean Expert, Diego Barros Arana, an intellectual of vast cultural background, sustains his reports on files and books, Perito (expert) Moreno again travels, inch by inch along the Cordillera, collecting innumerable geographical data on the terrain, that will be decisive for the arbitral decision.

In November 1902,King Edward VII of England, brings this problem to an end, which had taken the Chilean-Argentine relationship to a very dangerous point.

In 1903, as a reward for his service, the Government, awards him some land in the area of Nahuel Huapi Lake. He accepts the land and returns it, under the condition that it be preserved for future generations. His action, allowed the creation of the first Argentine **National Park**, and till the end of his days in 1919, he constantly advised the Government on the need of protecting and preserving natural resources.

Today, he rests, on an small island in Nahuel Huapi Lake, within the **National Park** that was created thanks to his generosity and wisdom.

### Perito Moreno Glacier

Like all the other Patagonian glaciers, (except for Cerro Tronador, near Bariloche) Perito Moreno Glacier, has its origins in the **Patagonian Icefield**, to which we will more extensively refer to in the chapter on **glaciation**.

*Geographical location:*
50° 29' South and 73° 03' West

*Velocity:*
1,7 m. per day in the middle and 0,45 m. on the sides.

The velocity was measured at about 5 km from the front in 1993 by scientists from the University of Sapporo - Japan and it approximately coincides with Raffo, Colki and Madejski's, that had measured it in 1952.

As we have said before, in the Chapter on Glaciology, the velocity of a glacier is a highly variable factor , that not only depends on the time of year, but on where it is measured, and even on the time of day when it is measured. The studies that were undergone at the Moreno, coincide with the ones carried out on the rest of the glaciers on the planet: the time of year it is the fastest corresponds to the end of spring/beginning of summer. During daytime, it will be faster during the first hours of the afternoon and slower at dawn.

*Lenght:* 30 km.

*Surface:* 257 km².

*Thickness:*

Both the latest studies that have been undergone on the Glacier as well as earlier ones on lateral moraines and in the forest surrounding the glacier, (trees over

500 years old have been found next to the ice) coincide on the fact that, contrarily to the rest of the glaciers in the area, PERITO MORENO has not greatly changed its ice mass in the last 500/1,000 years, and is not undergoing any alteration in its current thickness.

### Front Width:
4 km approximately.

### Equilibrium line:
About 1150 m.a.s.l.

**Front Status:** Stationary since about 1917.

Though the glacier front has had slight advancing and withdrawing movements since its first contact with land in 1917, we can affirm that it maintains the general aspect it had at the time.

And regarding the front, we would like to clarify some concepts that are sometimes confusing when we refer to the forward movement of a glacier: When we

Equilibrium line
(1150 m.a.s.l.)

**Perito Moreno Glacier**

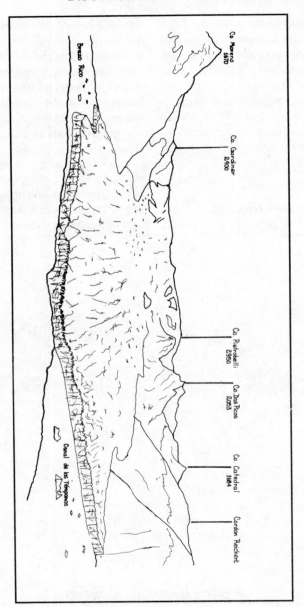

say that a glacier moves forward or withdraws, we are only referring to its front line, because as we have already mentioned, in all glaciers, ice is constantly undergoing a sliding or deformating advancing movement.

The factor that will provoke that advancing or withdrawing movement, will be the positive or negative relation between the ice that comes from the upper basins and the loss due to fusion, evaporation or ice falls at the lower basins.

*Front Height Above Lake Level:* from 50 to 70 meters.

*Maximum Basin Height:* Cerro Pietrobelli (2950 m.a.s.l.)

*Lake Depth:* The depth of Brazo Rico was only measured once, (Hauthal 1900). The maximum depth found was 137 m.

*Lake Height Above Sea Level:* 185 m.

*Lake Water Temperature:* from 4 to 6 C°.

*Water Color:* The characteristic milkish color of the Lake is due to suspended mineral particles in the water, that due to their microscopic size, do not sediment on the bottom.

Though the glacier front has slightly oscillated coming forth and wthdrawing later, since its first contact with land in 1917, we could affirm that it keeps the general aspect it had at the time.

We would like to clarify some concepts that sometimes are confusing regarding these movements: when we say that a glacier spreads or withdraws, we are only referring to the front line of the glacier, because as we have said before, in all glaciers, ice is in constant movement, due to sliding or defomation effects.

The factor that will make the glacier come forth or withdraw itself, will be the relationship, positive or negative, between the amounts of ice that come from the upper area, and the amounts loss due to evaporation or melting in the lower areas.

*Color of Ice:* When we contemplate the glacier, the deep blue color of the ice calls our attention. As we have said before, ice is but compacted snow. In this compacting process, the internal structure of the molecules of the snow evolves and transforms itself into a different body (ice), whose new light refraction planes, precisely reflect the blue color. ( Let's recall that all natural elements absorb a series of colors from the spectrum and reflect another, that is precisely the one we see).

Going back to the ice, the greater the compactness, the bluer the color, as it is easily seen while examining the glacier front and comparing its upper and lower zones.

## A Bit of History

Curiously –for he did not mention it in his reports– Perito Moreno, did not see the glacier, though in his 1876 exploration he was very close to it. His interest in the area at the time, was to verify if the Rico Arm belonged to Argentino Lake, which was achieved by traveling the Canal de los Tempanos a little to the west of today's town of **Punta Bandera**, where he planted a flag –therefore the name of the town–. On the other hand, they reached the other end of today's Rico Arm, where the entrance to the **National Park** is.

• In 1879. Juan Tomas Rogers, English Captain of the Chilean Navy, in an expedition from Punta Arenas, would be the first explorer to mention the glacier and name it: he called it Francisco Vidal Gormaz Glacier after the Director of the Hidrographic Office of the Chilean Navy, who had sponsored the expedition.

• Years later, Hauthal, adscript to the Argentine Limit Commission, called it Bismarck after the Prusian Chancellor. This name is still found in some German and Chilean maps.

• Lieutenant Iglesias, in charge of certain studies for the Argentine Hidrographic Institute, names it, in 1899, after Perito Moreno, which is the definite name of the glacier.

From then on, it has been visited by mountain climbers, explorers and scientists. From them, we have been able to keep track of its evolution, firstly regarding its great spread since the beginning of the century and later, once its front became stable, the phenomenon produced by its different ruptures:

• In 1900, the glacier front was 750 m from the coast of the Magellan Peninsula.

• In 1908, 350 m.

• In 1914, 100 m.

• In 1917, it touched Magellan Peninsula for the first time, opening again a few weeks later without major consequences.

• We do not have much data until 1926, when the Geologist E. Feruglio takes down the following information he had collected from the people of the area: "... the channel between the glacier and the shore of Cerro Buenos Aires, is wide enough to allow a boat sail through, without being endangered by the waves the ice blocks produce when falling from the steepy glacier front."

• In 1928, Father Agostini, who besides being a great Patagonian mountain climber pioneer, left us a very valuable photographic file on his expeditions, took pictures of the glacier that allow us to infer that the width of the channel at the time was about 150 m.

• Again we lack data until 1935, when we know the glacier closed for the second time, though again, as in 1917, for a short time.

• In the summer of 1939-40, the phenomenon which would call the attention first of glaciologists, and later, because of its spectacular beauty, of the whole world occured: that is the breaking of its front in Febuary 1940.

• In March 1942, the second breaking, the difference in level reached by the waters was 19 m, causing again great floods on the coast of the Rico Arm.

• After this breaking, and during ten years, the Glacier touched land several times producing various breakings (1947, 1949). In 1949 and 1950, greater snowfalls than usual are recorded. The glacier increases accordingly, and in July 1951, due to an enormous blocking,the Rico coasts begins to flood again.

With an almost 13 meter diference, the pressure makes the ice barrier explode and in March 1952, there is a new breaking.

• In September of the same year, the glacier closes again, and in March 1953 there was another breaking, the water level reaches 14.50 m.

• Three years later, at the beginnig of 1956, there is another breaking.

• Until 1966, the next times the glacier closed, there seems to have been no important floods.

• From 1970 to 1988, the glacier underwent several breakings, at a 2 to 4 year cycle (1970, 1972, 1975,1977,1980, 1984, and the last and most documented one was on February 17, 1988.

## The Breaking:
## The Whims of a Giant

The breaking of the Perito Moreno Glacier, is undoubtedly, one of the most impressive natural phenomenons that have been able to be contemplated in the last years. And when I say contemplate I am referring to the fact, that generally, it is not probable to be near and safe at the same time, when the great natural accidents occur (volcanos, floods, etc.)

Its fame has crossed the border lines and during the last breaking in 1988, televisions around the world patiently waited, some for months, to be able to film the event, that only lasted 24 hours. The easy access to the glacier, allowed hundreds of people to contemplate from a privileged natural view point, the development of the harmless cataclysm.

It is usually heard, that the breaking of the Moreno Glacier is a phenomenon that repeats its self cyclicly every 3 or 4 years. As we have seen above, that regularity has only occured in the last years. Just by looking at the breaking list that is detailed on the previous pages of this book, you can see that this is a wrong idea. The most recent prove, is found in the fact that since the last breaking in 1988, up to now (1993) there has not been another one. The glacier has closed, but it was not solidly enough to dam the water of the Rico Arm, that immediately found its way through boring a tunnel.

Another commom mistake about the glacier and its breaking, is to consider it unique in the world. A very close case of breaking is found in the Plomo Glacier, in the high basin of the Mendoza River, that in 1934, when blocking the course of the river, it produced a 40 m dike, whose stress bore a tunnel in the glacier, which produced alluviums that destroyed the Transandean Railway from Mendoza to Santiago. Fortunately, the Glacier began to withdraw, a short time later, not producing any more catastrophes.

Another phenomenon that is very similar to the Moreno's, happened at the end of the XIX century, in the Simadal Valley, in Norway. After repeated floods, for several years, in the area, due to successive breakings, a relieve tunnel was built through the rock, to avoid the level increase. The problem seemed to have been solved, but in 1937, the ice wall broke out, producing a new catastrophe down the river.

And speaking about catastrophes, the Moreno, during its first flood in 1939, covered the coastal lands of the Rico Arm, whose pastures were considered among the best in the region. This obliged some of people to abandon their farms, that represented many years of hard work and effort, as the floods came closer. From the road, toward the glacier, and just past the **National Park** entrance, even today the remains of the abandoned houses can still be seen, on the other side of the Lake.

In the presence of the relentless swell of the water, the Argentine Navy sends two planes to bomb the contact zone, with no positive result: the ice does not move an inch and the water keeps on rising.

After that, various solutions, one more impractible than the other, are proposed: one of them consists of trying the use of black bodies (soot, coloring) to accelerate the ice melting, by increasing the solar ray absorption. This method had been experimented by Russian scientists in the Tibetan glaciers. After complicated formulas, they come to the conclusion, that not less than 4 years would be needed to melt the ice blockade!

Somebody also took the trouble of calculating, mathematically, the amount of petroleum needed to burn the contact tongue: not less than 2700 tons.

Another solution, would be a tunnel through the rock, that had been used by Norwegians in the Simadal Valley: 500000 m³ would have to be moved, at a place where there was yet no road.

All the human solutions were impracticable, at last it was

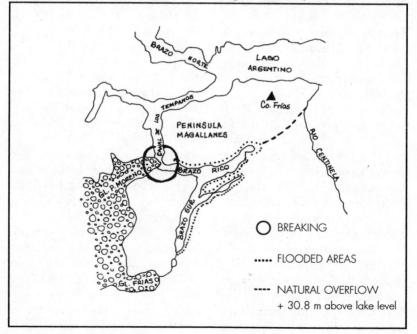

○ BREAKING

····· FLOODED AREAS

---- NATURAL OVERFLOW
+ 30.8 m above lake level

Nature itself that came to the rescue. Nature had blocked the way and a time later had opened it again, as it had been doing the successive years, that the ice wall had blocked the natural outlet of the Rico Arm.

### The scheme of a breaking

When the **glacier**, reaches the **Magellan Peninsula**, it forms a natural ice dam, that completely obstructs communication between the **Rico Arm** and the **Iceberg Channel** (Canal de los Témpanos). The water from Argentino Lake continues running toward the sea along the Santa Cruz River, whilst the **Rico Arm**, that has been isolated from the Lake, keeps on collecting water (rainwater, snow and ice meltwater...) and the level starts to rise.

The water level increase, starts to produce pressure on the ice dam. Under this pressure, little by little, water begins to filter through and to bore the ice at its weakest point, that coincides with the point where it touches land. Once the first crack is open, the water that runs through accelerates the melting of the frozen barrier. This opens a tunnel through it, that becomes bigger and bigger, due to the water that flows through, until it completely collapses. When this happens, the **Rico Arm** communicates again with **Argentino Lake**, through the channel that was opened between the Glacier and the coast.

When the glacier front comes forward again over the Channel, and touches the coast again, the process of the next breaking begins.

The difference of level of the **Rico Arm**, needed to produce a breaking, has notedly varied on the different occasions: from 13 meters in 1952, to 25 m, in 1988.

### Causes

The Moreno Glacier is one of the glaciers that has exceptionally spread in this century, in a zone where the tendency has been of a general withdrawal. (Actually, its front line has not changed greatly, since 1917, we could say it is in equilibrium) The other exception in the area, is Glacier Pio XI, that flows toward the Pacific, also from the South Patagonian Icefield and that has been tearing down the adjacent forest on its way like a monumental bulldozer.

The causes for this spread, have had different explanations according to the specialists: In Glaciology, as in the rest of the human knowledge, for each specialist with a theory, there is another one just as specialized, with another different one. Though none have been able to be proved, we will mention **Raffo**, **Colqui** and **Madejki's** theories, who in 1952 underwent the most complete survey on the glacier. According to them, the principal cause of the important spread of the glacier, would be due to the fact it had captured the nourishing basin of its neighbor, the Frias Glacier. This was corroborated by the fact that the latter had had an important withdrawal in this century compared to the rest of the glaciers of the area. This could be due to the seismicity of he area. Other secondary causes, according to the same authors, could be the abundant snowfall at its nourishment basin. These authors also calculated the highest flood level of the Rico Arm: If the water pressure was not able to break the ice dam, the Rico Arm would naturally drain along the Centinela River basin, when surpassing 30.8 meter beyond its normal level.

If it is difficult to know the causes the provoked the Moreno's behavior, it is even more difficult to try to forecast its future. Will it continue breaking? Will it keep on spreading? Or will the general heating up of the Planet, today's apparent cause of so many ecologic calamities, make the glacier withdraw, as almost all the rest of them in the world do at present? These are enigmas that Nature will reveal when the time comes.

# UPSALA GLACIER

Since, together with the Moreno, this is the most visited Glacier of the region, we would like to include a brief comment about this other glacier in this book.

The Upsala Glacier, owes its name to the Swedish City whose University sponsored the first glaciological survey of the region in 1908, and precisely this glacier was included in the objectives of this study.

It has two terminus tongues of about 4 km width each. Only the western tongue can be seen from the lake excursion). Its surface is 870 km$^2$ and its length 60 km, that makes it the longest of the Patagonian Icefield and hence of South America. The front height is approximately 60 meters above the lake level.

The top part is so flat, that it was chosen by the Antartic Command of the Argentine Army as a training zone for their dotations appointed to Antartica. The DC-3 plane that landed on the glacier is exhibited today at the Aeronautics Museum at the Domestic Airport of Buenos Aires (Jorge Newbery Airport).

Its velocity at the front, that was measured in November 1990 at a 4 day interval, was 3.6 meters per day. The authors of the study, (P. Skvarca and Aniya) point out that these exceptionally fast velocities,could be caused by abnormal rain conditions, wind and high temperatures recorded during the survey, that would have provoked an increase in the basal water flow of the glacier, that as we have seen, is one of the causes that increase the glacier's velocity.

Contrarily to what happens with the Moreno, that is characterized for its stability, the Upsala Glacier in the last years, has shown a very particular behavior regarding its front position:

• Between 1968 and 1970, the eastern part of its front came forward 150 m while the western one withdrew 300.

• Between 1970 and 1978, the eastern part came forward 250 m more and the western one withdrew a little.

• Later, the glacier began to withdraw, specially on its east part, at a 700 m per year average, during the 1981 and 1984 period. (In 1982, an inhabitant of the zone told the authors above mentioned, that was the warmest summer he could recall and that the lake at the time was full of icebergs).

• From then on, till 1990, the glacier has withdrawn on both sides at a 200 m rate a year approximately.

• From 1990 to 1993 again there was a great withdrawal: 400 m. per year along all its front, losing up to 1000m in the winter of 1992.

As it may be inferred from the above data, the Upsala Glacier's behavior, during the last years, has been highly unstable, though its general trend, has been to withdraw, which has emphasized from 1990 to 1993.

The studies that were undergone in 1993, have showed surprising results specially regarding its thickness: the glacier had lost 11 m per year at 1 km from the front, an amount which is considered the largest measure of all the glaciers on the planet in the last 30 years.

After its last great spread, which left us the Punta Bandera moraines, and its subsequent withdrawal, the Upsala Glacier has had very small spreads in recent years, and whose traces can be seen in the forests on its right side.The last spread had its peak in 1800 of our age, and that corresponds with numerous glacier spreads in Europe, which was called "the Little Ice Age".

One of the most beautiful spectacles that the Upsala grants us with, is that of the enormous icebergs that after falling off the glacier front, drift along, pushed by the winds along the North Arm and later down the Argentino Lake, till they sometimes anchor at the farthest end of the lake, where the sun, rain and wind end up melting them.

# GEOLOGY OF THE TERRITORY

150 million years ago, the Austral Patagonia was still a plain. The Andes did not exist and the damp air of the Pacific, blew with no obstacles all over today's steppe. At the time, it was a jungle, whose trees, petrified at present by the subsequent volcanic ashes, were over 25 m high and 3 m. diameter. They were the predecesors of the current araucarias in Northern Patagonia, and some of those specimens can be seen in the Petrified Forests of Jaramillo and Sarmiento (North of Santa Cruz Province and South of Chubut).

The Earth's enormous volcanic activity at the time, launched huge amounts of ashes into space, that were carried by the winds and finally settled in suc-cessive layers. After the fall, **the ashes gradually became compact**, be it because they were pasty and hot, or due to subsequent compacting processes: rain, chemical processes, etc.

Anyway, the fact is that they became solid rock, that for a long time was thought to be lava. Today, we know that it is volcanic tufa, that was formed as we have described above and whose thickness is 500 meters on top of a previous rock base, not yet very well known today.

After the depositing of the porphyritic complex, as the above mentioned deposits were called, was over, the next geological episode in Patagonia occurs in the Higher Jurassic and Cretaceous, that is, a time interval that began 140 million years ago and finished 80 million years ago.

During this period of time, today's Patagonian plateaus **sank**, thus allowing the invasion of ocean water, and forming the **Marine Complex** with its fossils (Belemnites, Ammonites, etc). The sea ingresion came from the Pacific, covering the area that would later become the Cordillera (remember the Cordillera was not yet formed at the time).

After this marine ingresion, the water withdrew for a short time and later a **New Marine Invasion** followed toward the end of the Cretaceous (some 70 million years ago), new sand and conglomerate layers sedimented on the ground, during this period.

When the Crestaceous was over, all these previous sediments start to become compact and fold: the **Andean Orogenic Cycle,** the creator of the Cordillera, begins. By the Oligocene (30 million years ago), the Cordillera had already risen, the **Last Marine Ingresion** begins, leaving in the landscape a new sediment layer, this time of a volcanic nature.

After this last Tertiary deposit, the Cordillera and the continent kept on **rising**, thus avoiding new oceanic invasions. Rivers originated in the Cordillera, wearing the land on their way to the Atlantic and thus forming the beginning of today's valleys, that the glaciers would later deepen, working on the landscape as a gigantic flexible file.

The last great geological event in the zone was the **intrusion**. Magmatic masses rose from within the earth and through the sedimentary rocks previously formed. As they slowly cooled off they originated the granitic batholith, that subsequent glacial erosion would gradually model, till forming the vertical needles, that today are a challenge for the best mountain climbers of the world, and produce indescribable feelings to those who approach them.

The best known formations of the kind in our zone are Macizo del **Fitz-Roy** (16 million years old) and **Paine** (12 million years old).

The following great alterations in the landscape would come with the glaciations, a phenomenon that is more extendedly developed in another chapter.

| AGE | PERIOD | STARTED (Million years ago) |
|---|---|---|
| QUATERNARY | *HOLOCENE*.................................. 0,01<br>*Man* appears in Patagonia<br>*PLEISTOCENE* ............................. 2<br>Great *glaciations* | |
| TERTIARY or CENOZOIC | *PLIOCENE*.................................... 7<br>First glaciation know in Patagonia<br>3,5 million years ago<br>*MIOCENE* ..................................... 22<br>Magmatic intrusions.<br>Formation of *Paine* and *Fitz-Roy*<br>*OLIGOCENE* ................................. 37<br>New Marine Invasion<br>*EOCENE* ........................................... 53<br>*PALEOCENE* ................................. 65<br>The Andes start to rise | |
| SECONDARY or MESOZOIC | *CRETACEOUS* ............................. 136<br>Sinking of the plateaus<br>*Marine Invasion*<br><br>*JURASSIC* ..................................... 190<br>Volcanic activity – Compacting of ashes<br>*Prophiritic Complex*<br>*TRIASSIC*...................................... 225 | |
| PRIMARY or PALEOZOIC | *PERMIAN*...................................... 280<br>*CARBONIFEROUS*...................... 350<br>*DEVONIAN* ................................... 400<br>*SILURIAN* ..................................... 435<br>*ORDOVICIAN* .............................. 500<br>*CAMBRIAN*................................... 570 | |
| PRECAMBRIAN | *PROTEROZOIC* .......................... 2000<br>Fungus, worms, jellyfish<br>*ARCHEOZOIC*............................. 3500<br>Life begins in the seas<br>*PRECAMBRIAN*.......................... 4600<br>Formation of earth's crust | |

# ONCE UPON A TIME... THE ANDES

In the beginning, 500 million years ago, Pangea was the only continent on earth, that later divided into two others: Laurentia in the north and Gondwana in the south. The latter comprised the emerging lands that today we know as South America, Africa, Antarctica, Australia and India and which also kept on separating among one another, resembling gigantic floating rafts on the astenosphere, a kind of viscous and semifluid substratum that surrounds the earth under its solid crust or lithosphere.

As South America drifted westward, it encountered another enormous plate that traveled in the other sense known as the Nazca plate. From the collision between two masses of such magnitud, no gentle situation could turn out: the phenomena this encounter provoked (and that today still continues), are one of the most convulsive chapters in the geological history of our agitated planet: the formation of the Andes Cordillera.

The Nazca plate, denser and heavier than the Southamerican one, started to sink toward the center of the earth while the Southamerican remained on the surface, but with great alterations on its west side: the friction caused by the rubbing of the two plates against each other, generated very high tempertures, as well as the inevitable fracture of the crusts due to the enormous pressure. It allowed the magma to rise to the surface all along the contact zone between the plates, forming innumerable volcanoes that casted huge amounts of material into the atmosphere during their constant eruptions, that later when they settled on the surface, started forming the base of the future cordillera.

But vulcanism was not the only generating force of the Andes: the plates did not simply slide against each other, but when they collided they pressured, twisted and convoluted enormous rock masses, rising them slowly and into successive folds thousands of meters away from their original position.

The finding of marine fossils at great heights confirm these verticle movements of the crust of the earth, a phenomenon that Darwin had already suggested during his expedition from Santiago de Chile to Mendoza crossing the cordillera and that was only demonstrated well within the XX century with the theory that derives from the continental plates. Today this theory helps us understand the frequent seismic and volcanic activity that continues occurring along the contact lines of the different plates. Though Patagonia is not a specially active zone in this sense, the eruption of the Hudson volcano ( Chile ) in 1991 reminded us the processes and phenomena that keep on happening under our feet.

# HISTORY

## American Populating

There are many theories that have tried to explain the origen of the populating of America: Egyptians that arrived on rafts from the Atlantic, Polynesians from the Pacific... There were also the Americanists that taken by their patriotic zeal, claimed that the origen of humanity lie in American lands.

Nevertheless, today, the most accepted theory, not excluding the others, is that the first people of America came on foot, crossing the Behring Strait between Alaska and Siberia approximately 20,000 years ago. In that time, due to a great glaciation that was reaching its peak, the sea level was about 100 meters lower than today's, which al-lowed men and animal of that time to pass through places that today are covered with water.

18,000 years ago, the glaciers began to withdraw, leaving the way toward the south clear for humans, that 8,000 years later had already reached the south-ern part of the Continent, be-cause the oldest remains to be found in Tierra del Fuego date back about 10,000 years.

Numerous rupestrian paint-ings have been found all over Patagonia, but due to their num-ber and state of conservation, the most famous are the ones of **La Cueva de las Manos** (Hands Cave), in the northeast of the province of Santa Cruz; curi-ously, they are very similar to certain rupestrian European paintings from the time of Cro magnon. The hand drawings are made by placing the open hand on the rock and then by blowing, probably with a cane, colored pigments over it so as to leave the negative of the hand printed on the wall. There are also some scenes that represent the guanaco hunt. The oldest findings of la Cueva de las Manos, date back to 9000 years ago.

## The Tehuelches

Nothing was known about the Patagonian man until 1520, when Antonio Pigafetta, the meticulous chronicler of Magellan's expedition, tells us about some pleasant giants dressed in guanaco furs from head to toes.

These aborigines' kind and trusting character, would lead them, from then on, to collaborate with the white men whenever necessary, and the latter did need their help: they were the ones that informed and escorted Antonio de Viedma's expedition (1782) during the days of the colony; after the first Chilean and Argentine settlements were established, they were the ones to approach the newcomers and start a permanent and always increasing trade: guanaco meat and leather, fox and skunk skins, ostrich feathers were all swapped for tobacco, chambergos, alcohol, tools, flour... Since they were great connoisseurs of the area, they would also lead the settlers in their explorations to the inlands.

The first encounters between the two cultures were not very traumatic. It will be when the land begins to have owners, that these will start an inevitable and deadly struggle with those who had always roamed the region with no sense of property whatsoever, except for their horses and dogs.

*The Origen of the Name:* The most common version, to why they were called **Patagones**, and hence the name of **Patagonia** for the region where they lived, was attributed to Magellan's men, on account of the natives' enormous feet; and apart from their considerable height, they were all wrapped up in guanaco furs. Nevertheless, according to the most accepted version of the specialists on the subject, the name Patagones would be due to a physical resemblance of the Indians, with Patagon, the principal character of one of the most popular gentlemanly novels from the beginning of XVI century. Let's recall that these novels were real "best sellers" at the time and their characters were as popular as our TV heroes.

Another version that has achieved some followers among the specialists on the matter is, that when Magellan's men saw the poverty and Spartan simplicity the Tehuelches lived in, they called them "Patagones" after the Portuguese currency "Patacao" that was of little value at the time.

Perito Moreno, came to the conclusion after measuring the Tehuelches of the Santa Cruz River area, that the size of their feet did not justify their nickname, because though they were considerably tall, their feet were small in relation to their height

***Habits and Customs:*** Wherever their name came from, the fact is they called themselves **Aonikenk**. Of course, nobody at the time thought of asking them why; —this was a very common characteristic during the civilizing colonizing history of the world— They basically lived on the hunting of guanacos and choikes (ñandues). They also gathered roots, herbs, berries and seeds, and made flour out of them.

As nomads, they roamed all the Patagonian plateau, from the Cordillera to the Atlantic, following the guanaco herds. Their social organization was formed by a group of several families under the leadership of a chief. Each group's territory, was well delimited, and the trespassing of those limits was the cause for many struggles among them. Their favorite camping sites (Aikes) according to the season and the concentration of the game, have remained to this day in several locations of today's regional toponymy: Guer-aike, Tapi-aike, Chali-aike... We know nothing about their exact number, though it seems that their great mobility, did not allow the formation of human concentrations of the kind of the Precolombian civilizations as the ones of Perú or México. The 1869 census, reveals 24.000 in all Patagonia, and the one in 1895, only 5.500.

Though the exactness of the censuses of that time was very far from today's, and therefore the figures are quite relative; the drastic decrease in number in such a short period of time, gives us an idea of what happened to those "pleasant giants" in contact with more "civilized" races.

But let's return to the Tehuelches while they still ex-

## THE WORLD ACCORDING TO THE TEHUELCHES

**Kooch**. the creator, always existed; one day, sad and lonely, he began to cry. His tears created the sea, his sighs the wind, and his hands the sun, which dissipated the dark. The sun, the clouds and the wind were later arranged by the creator. He made an island rise in the midst of the sea, where he placed the animals.

To lighten the earth while the sun rested, he created the moon, that would later end up having an affair with the sun-king in complicity with the clouds.

While the sun and the moon loved each other, time fecundated the night, who consequently gave birth to malefic spirits and gigantic monsters that lived in the mountains.

One of these giants, **Noshtex**, kidnapped a cloud, took her to his cavern, and from that wedding **Elal** would be born, the principal hero of the Tehuelche mythology, and the creator of men.

Through the wind, Noshtex learnt that his son would become more powerful than him, so by all means he tried to kill him. In the end, Elal would be saved by a small rodent, the tucu-tucu, who hid him in its cave.

When the divine hero could no longer remain hidden, the tucu-tucu organized a meeting with all the animals, which protected Elal's escape, on a swan's back, to a region known today as Patagonia.

The swan landed on the **Chaltén**, where **Elal** descended to earth.

Shortly after, the cold and the snow attacked him, so he protected himself by striking two stones against each other and thus he created fire..

When the condor informed Noshtex, the evil father, of his son's new residence, **Noshtex** moved to Patagonia in his attempt to eliminate his offspring. To defend himself from his father, **Elal** will create the forests and men (**Chonek**), who he will also teach to hunt with a bow and arrow.

As a result, of a terrible fight with a giant his father had sent, **Lake Cardiel** would be formed,- a lake of bitter waters due to the sweat of the two gladiators. During the fight, the Chonek or Tehuelches, were unfaithful to their creator and took his opponent's side, and though Elal forgave them, he was disappointed by his children, and decided to leave.

His mission was over. The men had learnt hunting techniques, the natural obstacles had been overcome; the only thing left for Elal to do, was to leave them a protecting spirit that would watch over them during lifetime and would accompany them after death to their judgment before Elal; after which, they would be able to get together to chat with their friends, around the fire that never goes out.

One morning, in silence, he left to the East ,on a swan's back, just like he had arrived; and he rested on the islands that rose far away, over there, where the arrows wounded the sea.

isted. Physically, all the accounts agree that they were tall ( the men 1,70/1,80 m and the women a little less ) and strong. Another feature that called the attention, was the health and whiteness of their teeth, that seemed to be achieved by chewing some kind of resin, extracted from the roots of the incense. Both men and women smeared their faces with ocher or black soil mixed with cooked marrow from the bones of hunted animals, to thus protect themselves from the rigor of the wind and the sun. On special occasions, such as feasts and ceremonies, they would use plaster or paint to draw lines and marks on their chests.

The chores were well defined between the two sexes: while hunting was the men's main occupation, the women made quillangos (blankets made of guanaco skins), built the huts on the campsites, fetched water and firewood, wove hairbands and sashes.

The marriges were always freely arranged, and no woman was obliged to accept a suitor she did not like. Poligamy was allowed, though most men had only one woman, and rarely two or more.

Their hunting weapon was the boleadora: two or three round stones lined in leather and held togeher with ostrich tendons, that became mortal projectiles in their hands; they could reach a running guanaco from more than 50 meters distance. After becoming acquainted with the white man they started substituing the stones with metal balls that were shiny and easier to find among the bush or the gravel in case they should miss a shot. They were skillful horsemen and their itinerant lives obliged them to learn how to ride before they learned to walk. When they traveled from one camp to another, the caravan of women and children would usually follow the easy trail while the men deviated to thus round up possible groups of guanacos or choikes. They all met at the new predetermined camp where the women were awaiting them with the huts ready and the fire burning for the daily meal.

When a Thuelche died, he was buried in a sitting position facing the east. His horses were killed and eaten by his and his widow's relatives. The latter, together with her closest friends would sing endless songs and laments. Once the ceremony was over, the dead one was not mentioned again and any allusion to

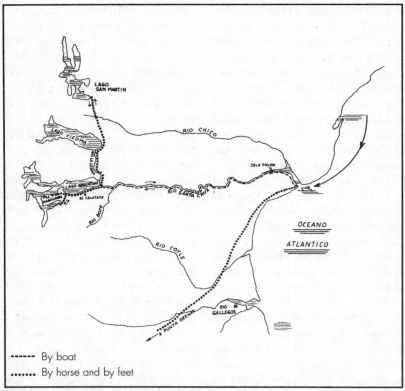

------ By boat
....... By horse and by feet

**Exploration of Moreno (1876 / 1877)**

him was avoided.

These were the people who lived along the coast of the **Argentino Lake** until the first Europeans arrived. Today, only a century after the white man began populating Patagonia, the Tehuelches are completely extinct: alcohol, new diseases they had no defenses against, the killings - some of the new land and estancia owners would pay for every Indian ear delivered to them, as it is still done today with the puma skins- and most of all, a sedentary culture and the extensive cattle raising, so completely different from theirs, ended up by destroying them.

As in all the mythologies, the Tehuelches found many of the explanations to the natural world that surrounded them, in theirs. We will quote only some in this paper:

**The Southern Cross** one of the many signs that **Elal** left, to orientate his Tehuelchian friends on their last journey toward the stars.

**The sea and the wind** were **Kooch's** tears and sighs, the supreme creator.

**The ñandu cannot fly** because he was punished by ELAL for arriving late to the animal meeting where they planned his escape.

**The skunk's nauseous smell** would be due to the animal's treason, when the meeting mentioned above was held.

**The flamingo** was given dawn's color as a reward to his loyalty.

**The "red breast"** (Long Tailed Meadowlark), which during the meeting had distracted the giants with his singing, was wounded and killed by them, later **Elal** resurrected it, and rewarded him with the splendid red color of its breast.

**The red skies at dawn** would be **Elal's** cloud-mother's blood when she was killed by his father **Noshtex**.

## Explorers

Except for the frustrated Spanish attempts to colonize Patagonia at Cabo Virgenes (1584), Puerto Deseado, (1780) and Puerto San Julián (1781 and 1790) until well in the XIX century, Patagonia was only visited by sailors that came to shore searching for water stations or transitory shelter, against the fearful tempests so frequent in this zone.

The first Europeans to come close to Lake Argentino were the restless **Fitz-Roy** and **Darwin**, that during their exploration trip around the world in 1834, went up the Santa Cruz River, and were about to reach the Lake, but got as far as today's Bote River. But the endless plain that still stretched out before them and which they called "the Plain of Mystery" discouraged them; the strong river current and their provisions that were running short finally made them turn around and go down the river in the same boats that they had so difficultly towed up river from the shore. Nevertheless, their names would forever remain in the region: **Fitz-Roy** in the peak that later his admirer, **Perito Moreno**, would name after him, and **Darwin**, due to his innumerable and acute observations on the flora and fauna, was inmortalized in numerous scientific names of many Patagonian species. Even the ship they sailed, (**H.M.S. Beagle**) remains in the topography of the region naming the channel between Tierra del Fuego and Navarino Island.

In 1859, Commander Luis Piedra Buena, settled near the mouth of the Santa Cruz River, inaugurating the Argentine settling in the region. A legendary and admirable pioneer for his time, Piedra Buena trades with the Indians, hunts sea wolves, rescues ships and, as a naturally bred explorer, organizes and finances expeditions. During one of them, in 1867, an Englishman, Gardiner, together with three sailors of the same nationality, are the first white men to reach Argentino Lake. Nevertheless they thought they had reached the Viedma Lake, a place they had heard of, known since 1782, after don Antonio de Viedma's expedition, who in time of the Colony and guided by Indians, had crossed the Patagonia steppe, from the Atlantic up to the Cordillera looking for wood to build with. Due to the time of the season, they were forced to turn back before achieving there

goal, but his name remained forever more related to one of the great Patagonian lakes. The British sailors, contrarily to what their job could make you suppose, went on land and on horse back, continued along the southern shore of the Lake, till they reached today's Roca Lake and the Rico Arm.

In 1873, another expedition, under the leadership of Captain Feilberg, this time going up the river, finally discovers the sources of the Santa Cruz River in the Lake, though like his predecessors, he also mistakes it for the Viedma Lake.

The expedition under **Francisco Pascasio Moreno** leadership, later known as Perito Moreno, would not only be the one to reach the lake going up river in 1876/77, but also the first to carryout an extense visit of the zone, from which several very important conclusions were made, not only geographically speaking but politically as well: later on it would be the Perito Moreno's great knowledge of the zone that would allow him to defend the Argentine sovereignty in that zone, precisely due to that great knowledge. A brief review of his life and work will be found in the pages dedicated to the Perito Moreno Glacier.

Once the cartography of the zone was finished, and many interrogations answered, other more scientific related expeditions were undergone. The populating of the area would still take some time. The border conflict with Chile discouraged the potencial settlers.

### The settling of Lago Argentino

When the problem with the neighboring country was partially solved after the the 1881 Treaty, the up to then Patagonian desert that till then had only seen the coming of explorers, started to receive is first populators.

The times when **Darwin** had made his famous statement on Patagonia. **"The curse of sterility covers these lands"**, was long forgotten. Wool was permanently better quoted in the world and now a score of farms were sprouting in the once desert steppes; adventurers, outlaws and immigrants from all over the world came to try luck. The first sheep were brought from the Falkland Islands, and little by little the lands closest to the coast were occupied, because the sea was the only access to these

regions, and its ports the only outlet for its production.

Some data will enlighten on the sheep raising outburst in the zone at the time: In 1895 there were 370,000 sheep heads in the Province of Santa Cruz; twenty years later almost 4,000,000, the figure had increased tenfold.

We will extend ourselves a little on this economic and social phenomenon that occurred all over the Austral Patagonia, in the chapter dedicated to the estancias (farms).

At the beginning of the current century, the people who wanted to settle down in this region had to go westward. Hence the first settlers of the Argentino Lake zone arrived, they were spread out on lands the government gave in concession, leasing or ownwership and that as time went by became the estancias that today populate the region.

They were real **"Farsouth"** pioneers, their lives were true examples of tenacity and sacrifice in taming these beautiful but inhospitable lands.

Toward 1925, Argentino Lake was completely surrounded by rural settlers spread out in about twenty estancias (farms), generally with good facilities; they

## ANDREAS MADSEN, AN AUSTRAL PIONEER

The best known pioneer of the zone, his life and personality can well serve as a symbol of the human kind that was needed to populate the Patagonia of that time, and of the difficulties and hardships the first settlers of the region underwent.

He was born in Denmark in 1881. His life resembles a tale of Dickens: he worked in the Jutland farms since he was 9 years old, in semislavery conditions, that were so common in today's very developed Scandinavian countries. At the age of 15, he ran away from home taking only what he had on, and finds the freedom he so eagerly longed for at sea. He enlisted on several vessels, and debarked at the port of la Boca, where he decides to try luck once again, in Argentina, the promise land of the beginning of the century, for all the miserable and undernourished Europeans.

As a skillful sailor he easily found a job with the Argentine Commission of Limits that was permanently traveling the Patagonian Cordillera and navigating its rivers and lakes, at the time. In 1903, he arrived at the Viedma Lake, where he meets a curious German character, a taxidermist by profession and a gold searcher by vocation, who invites him to stay in the zone, a proposal that our Dane does not take long to accept "...space with no limits and lands with no owners", at last his childhood dreams had come true.

What he had probably not dreamt of, was that his knew partner would leave him all alone in that spot while he went to the coast, 400 km away for provisions and, where the taxidermist adventurer planned to arrive in a month's time. He would hunt choikes on his way and buy the provisions with the money he would collect from selling the feathers. Unfortunately for Madsen, the month turned into half year, because the German drank up the money from the feathers in every saloon he found on his way.

During that hard Patagonian baptism, Madsen had to survive like a real Robinson Crusoe, in the midst of a deserted island; that is, the place where today the small town of El Chalten lies. He tells us in his narration's, that the fox would lie around the bonfire, awaiting a piece of meat and that the huemuls would trustingly graze in the neighboring meadows oblivious of the newly arrived animal. To survive, he built a hut made of logs and he " bolea "guanacos the Tehuelche way, until his friend returns from the coast with the long dreamt of provisions.

English, Scandinavian, Germans and very few Chileans and

Argentines, start to populate the Lake Viedma zone, at that time. Each one arrived with his implements, sheep, a troop of horses and mares, a couple of oxen, and would settle down wherever they found a piece of land that belonged to nobody and began their pioneering attempt: some would thrive, but most failed because of the winter, the pumas or the great wool companies, that at the beginning of the century had already started to occupy all the land that was fit for their insatiable appetites.

After the roaming of the Tehuelche tribes, now almost desegregated, the land saw a new kind of wanderer in seek of work, new lands, and in some cases shelter against unpaid debts with justice, that at the time, added up to two or three police posts on the coast. There was lots of work to be done and personnel was scarce; so nobody with two legs and two arms was questioned about his past.

At least once a year, they had to travel to the coast on wagons pulled by oxen, where they would sell the wool, leather and feathers, and would buy provisions. Madsen made this one month trip from his ranch on the foot of the cordillera several times, and with all the hardships, anecdotes and characters our pioneer described along those roads, endless adventure books could be written.

Besides working as a wagon driver, he accepted any occupation that allowed him to survive in the region at the time: horsebreaker, cattle driver, puma hunter... Due to his nobleness, intelligence and working capacity he became the administer of several neighboring estancias until he decided to have one of his own. He definitely settled down with his wife, and there his four children are born. As time went by, he was able to raise a flock of 2000 sheep, a respectable number if you take into account the difficult conditions of the land, the constant puma attacks, so very frequent in those places, and that the enduring pioneer would constantly hunt during the winter, following the fresh prints in the snow.

At that time, the isolated Patagonian estancias, and especially the ones in the cordillera region, obliged their dwellers to depend as little as possible on the outside world. Besides the cattle work, vegetables, cereal and grass were raised near the house, and all the implements for carpentry, iron works for everyday use, horseshoes, house furniture, wagons... were made in the warehouse.

He died in San Carlos de Bariloche, where his family had taken him two years before due to his illness. In 1977, thanks to the collaboration of the Argentine Air Force and National Gendarmerie, his remains were taken to the family cemetery on the estancia, by the de las Vueltas River, facing the Fitz Roy "...in the most beautiful place on Earth any man could choose to live on."

had big sheapshearing barns, houses for the workers and foremen, corrals, orchards and groves for protection against the wind. In the summer the territory would enliven with the arrival of the Chilean sheepshearing groups and some occasional visitors.

In 1934, there are already 1564 inhabitants in the area, more than half are foreigners. (specially Spaniards).

At the beginning,the wool production was taken to the Atlantic coast on oxen pulled wagons (you can still see a couple of them at the entrance of El Calafate), and from the 30's on, they were taken in motor vehicles.

## The Beginnings of El Calafate

At the beginning of the century, the region's transport (wool and hides to Rio Gallegos and other Atlantic Ports, foodstuff and household goods from there back to the Cordillera) was only done in wagons pulled by oxen.

The Patagonian trails had wagon stops every 3/4 leagues (20 km approximately), that was about a day journey for the wagons. These stopping places were located by streams, lagunas or other naturally protected spots. After a time, a general goods stores with a bar and a hotel would be built at the site.

The road from Rio Gallegos to Argentino Lake would divide in two at a ford along the Santa Cruz River, today called Charles Fuhr, after a settler of the area; the road to the right, after crossing the river by raft, continued northward coasting La Leona River toward the Viedma Lake up today's Route 40. The one to the left, went along the southern Lake shore toward the Cordillera. One of the stop stations, along the latter was by a stream, that due to the big calafate shrubs along its shores, ended up by being called El Calafate. Later on the wagon drivers also gave the overlooking mountain, the same name.

In 1913, the two first families settle down in the location and begin a boarding and grocery business on the road to the Cordillera. Long suffering Spanish immigrants, used to harder lands, after a few years of tilling the soil and working the alluvial plains around the stream, turned the place into a real paradise, where cereal, fruit and vegetables began to grow protected by poplar tree barriers.

In 1921/22, the region is agi-

Orquídeas

Chilco - *Fuchsia magellanica*

Anémona - *Anemone multifida*

Ourisia - *Ourisia alpina*

Violeta - *Viola maculata*

Aguila Mora (Juvenil) - *Geranoetus melanoleucus*

Pato Cuchara - *Anas platalea*

Cóndor - *Vultur gryphus*

Carancho - *Polyborus plancus*

Choique - *Pterocnemia pennata*

Guanaco - *Lama guanicue*

Pato Zambullidor - *Oxyura ferruginea*

Zorro Gris - *Dusicyon griseus*

tated by the general strike undergone by the Patagonian estancia workers. The government represes the strikers with great firmness. The final episode takes place in Estancia Anita, 30 km from Calafate, where the last opposing group is massacred after having surrendered to the troop. The inspirer and leader of the strike, a Spanish anarchist, was able to escape to Chile through the mountains, and after thousands of hardships, returned to Rio Gallegos 12 years later, from where he was expelled by the governor at the time, Governor Gregores. He died in Punta Arenas in 1963.

The point is, that all these events, hastened the authority's decision to create several towns in the interior of the province, among them "a place called El Calafate, south of Argentino Lake".

Finally, the town would be officially formed on December 7, 1927. In the coming years, it was provided of the principal services: school, police, doctor, post office, judge of peace...

In 1946, the town already had 368 inhabitants, and precisely, that same year Aeroposta Argentina −today's Aerolineas Argentinas after the merging with other air companies− began its commercial flights .

In 1950, the Administration of Los Glaciares National Parks, created in 1937, is set up in the town.

At the beginning of the 60's. National Parks opens a road up to the Perito Moreno Glacier, till then the only way to get to the Glacier was on horseback (Rio Mitre Division).

In 1969, now with 700 inhabitants, the Bank of the Province sets up a branch.

In 1972, the first touristic season is officially launched. The National Government assigned the town, an important amount of money to improve the touristic infrastructure: Hotels, Airport, the Punta Bandera Dock...

The road to the glacier, that till then had only been a trail for sturdy vehicles, is greatly improved; the Army builds articulated bridges over the streams, thus solving the problem of the great spring swells caused by ice melting and consolidating Calafate as the entrance toward the Cordillera.

In 1978, a Squadron of the National Gendarmerie, sets up an operative base for a number of preexiting posts along the Cordillera. Many of the gendarms, that came from the northern provinces, will later

**Longitudinal cutting of the Cordillera**

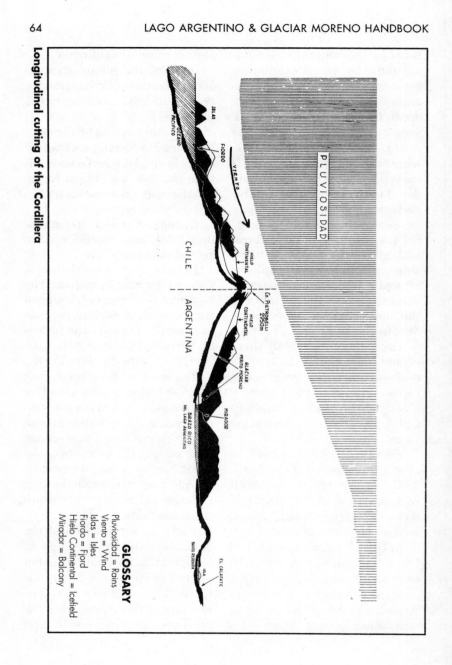

**GLOSSARY**

Pluviosidad = Rains
Viento = Wind
Islas = Isles
Fiordo = Fjord
Hielo Continental = Icefield
Mirador = Balcony

remain in town, and are one of the most important growth factors until Tourism arrived.

In the 70's, the Cattle Society, introduces some heads of "Hereford" breed in the region, that would later admirably adapt to the precordillera zone – hence increasing the possibilities of livestock raising in the zone– that had been till then, only limited to sheep raising.

As we have already said, at the beginning of the 70's, service and supply centers for the area are set up, and this would be the beginning of what later would become the principal cause of the economic take off of Calafate: Tourism.

At that time, there were only 7 small hotels of a very simple category, that would add up 50 rooms in all. The Provincial Government had just inaugurated the "Lago Argentino Touristic Complex" with the the first hotel of a higher category and some bungalows, that would add 30 rooms to the scarce lodging offer of the time.

Firstly, the domestic tourism,

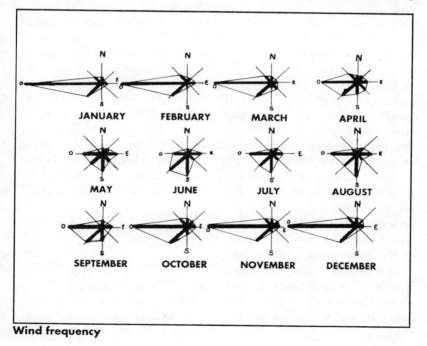

**Wind frequency**

and then in the 80's the international tourism discovers the natural wonders of the zone, that gradually become a classic in any South American touristic program.

Till then, the touristic service offer has constantly increased, and today (1999) Calafate has over 2000 beds, in all the categories, from a simple family house to a luxury hotel.

Another important step toward the tourism of the zone, has been the recent inauguration of the new paved airport, in May 1999.

## Climate

The territory of Argentino Lake, has several kinds of weather, that vary from the snowy area of the Cordillera, to the arid Patagonia steppe, in only a 200 km distance.

At the enormous Patagonian Ice Sheet, the annual snowfall reaches 5000 mm. Then it decreases a little to the East up to about 1500 mm, now as rainfall, at the farthest end of the lake channels (Mayo and Ameghino Fiords). This abundance of rains, allows the formation of thick forests adjacent to the sides of the glaciers.

From here on, always Eastward, a 30/40 km strip, still allows a forest formation that decreases in density and height in direct proportion to the decrease in rainfall. The limit to this strip is around Punta Bandera and Rio Mitre's mouth. The rainfall within this strip oscilates between 1000 and 500 mm annually.

To the East, rainfall decreases to about 300 mm, and the dry landscape of the steppe, only allows a very scarce vegetation of gramineous and xerophilous plants. The only exceptions, to this climate are found at the bottom of the lake and river basins, where though scarce rainfall, the ambient humidity and temperature are modified by the proximity to bodies of water. Regarding Calafate's specific case, the fact it is located on a northward declivity and due to the artificial protection given by its groves, allows it to benefit from a much milder microclimate than that of the surrounding plateaus.

### Situation:
Latitude: 50° 20' South
Longitude: 72° 18' West

### Elevations a.s.l.: 190 meters

### Mean Temperatures:
– Mean Minimum (July) -1.8
– Mean Maximum (Jan.) 18.6
– Mean Annual 7.2

*Day duration:*
Minimum (Jun 21) 9 hours
Maximum (Dec 21)16 1/2 hrs.

*Mean Rainfall:*
250 mm annual

*Windiness:*
Strong winds from the West during Spring and Summer, wind gusts up to 120 km/h specially during daytime.

We did not want to miss this chance to say a little more about the formation and dynamics of wind in Patagonia. Besides being the cause of many aspects of the landscape, it is also a legendary symbol of the region, that is always mentioned (and often exagerated on) in any description about the zone.

As we have already seen in the chapter on Glaciology, the wind currents blowing from the Pacific, are responsible for the successive formation, in Patagonia, first of the ice fields, then of the forests and finally of the steppes, if we travel from West to East.

On the other hand, these winds are predominant in the Austral Spring and Summer (see adjoining graph) due to the displacement of the great South Pacific anticyclone, which makes the latitudes included between 40° and 60° specially affected during these seasons.

Besides, the earth rotation creates a series of winds and marine currents on the planet, that in the Southern Hemisphere act as a great wind ring that blows from the West to the East, within the above mentioned latitudes.

We have also said, that the wind is predominant during the daytime: (" The wind appears at ten o'clock", according to an old Patagonian saying). This is because, as these Patagonian plateaus are enormous stepparian extensions, when the sun heats the land it produces a low pressure zone as the hot air rises. This allows the wind from the west, to accelerate even more its speed, as has been explained above. At night, when the land cools off, the inverse phenomenon occurs, thus "stopping" the winds.

---

(1) Thus the official name of the village is "El Calafate", in the area is simply known as "Calafate". In this book I've decided to use both denominations, as so valid is for me the official one, as the one created by the people in their everyday's life. Let the byzantine discussions lovers, find the final solution to the conflict

# FLORA

## A botanic look throughout the zone

As we have already said, rainfall rapidly decreases to the East, and thus determines several kinds of vegetation in the Argentino Lake zone, that we could divide into three zones:

**1- Stepperian zone:** Rainfall is less than 400 mm yearly, and the existing plants are low and generally thorny, adapted to such rigorous metereological conditions: strong winds, dryness, low winter temperatures...

**2- Pre-andean bush and transition forest:** Increased rainfall, allows a larger growth of the species that were already found in the latter and the growth of shrubs and trees, that announce the great Magellanic forest.

**3- Magellanic forest:** With an 800 to 2000 mm annual rainfall, this zone encloses the most western cordilleran forest that grows by the glaciers, and which forms a landscape that is seldom seen elsewhere. The limits of the forest are, firstly, the glaciers we have already mentioned, and secondly, height. Over approximately 800 m.a.s.l. trees begin to stunt, until they become creeping bushes and completely disappear toward 1000 m.a.s.l. The extreme weather conditions hardly allow vegetable life: only small plants and lichens that have adapted to the great temperature differences and the weight of snow. This latter biotic province is known as the Alpine Prairie or Height Desert.

As it is not our purpose to list

all the species of the zone in this paper, we will only include a brief list of the most easily observable ones, at the end of this chapter.

We, suggest, a kind of "botanic look" during the Perito Moreno Glacier excursion, an inevitable tour for all our visitors, and that precisely goes through the three vegetable provinces we have mentioned, that on the other hand, are common to all the Austral Patagonia.

# STEPPE

On leaving the town, the typical landscape of the Patagonian steppe already surrounds us: low xerophilous plants (adapted to living in dry places), among the gramineous, the yellowish **coiron** (1) stands out, that, in its four varieties, is the predominant plant of the steppe.

We also begin to see, **calafate** (2) bushes scattered everywhere (the town was named after the enormous bushes that grow in the area). In Spring, the bush is covered by bright yellow flowers, and toward the end of the Summer, its very sweet black blueish berries are ready to be gathered, to prepare a delicious jam.

The saying goes, that whoever eats calafate will return to Patagonia, so we recommend to those that undoubtedly want to return, to try it.

Twenty miles away from the town, on the shores of the Centinela River, another typical Patagonian steppe shrub, the **mata negra** (3) covers the zone.

As we continue Westward, other plants and shrubs start to appear: the **neneo** (4) a typical xerophilous plant of a semi-spherical shape and with big thorns, whose fruit, when eaten by the sheep, gives a strong taste to their meat; The **mata guanaco** (5) that is covered by small bright red flowers in Spring, the **paramela** (6) with strong resinous smelling leaves, the **romerillo** (7) which also has a particular smell.

In Spring, the **zapatitos de**

**la virgen** (8) and the **topa-topa** (9) are very frequent, and orna- ment the area with their bright colors.

# THE PRE-ANDEAN BRUSH AND THE TRANSITION FOREST

Forty km from Calafate we find the first mountains of the Cordillera: it is Sierra Buenos Aires. In the small canyons of the flanks nearest to the steppe, we observe a phenomenon that illustrates well on the relationship between vegetation and insolation: the slopes looking to the North are dry, while trees

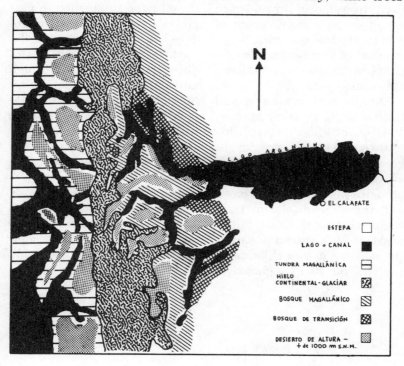

N

LAGO ARGENTINO

○ EL CALAFATE

ESTEPA

LAGO o CANAL

TUNDRA MAGALLÁNICA

HIELO CONTINENTAL - GLACIAR

BOSQUE MAGALLÁNICO

BOSQUE DE TRANSICIÓN

DESIERTO DE ALTURA — + de 1000 m s.n.m.

cover the ones looking to the South.

Just before entering the National Park, at about Rio Mitre, we find the first trees next to the route: they are **ñires** (10), one of the three Nothofagus original of the zone and that always mark the transition between the stepperian zone and the Magellanic Forest.

The Nothofagus are an endemic species of Patagonia, Tierra del Fuego, New Zealand, Australia and Tasmania, regions that, in remote times, were joined to the extreme south of America by the Antartica, forming part of Gondwana; a continent which began to divide itself 220 million years ago.

On the Ñire branches, and farther along on other species, we frequently find the **farolillos chinos** (11), that are bright green vegetable spheres. This is a kind of mizodendrum, a semiparasitic plant, that lacks roots, and therefore dwells in trees sucking part of their sap. Afterwards it elaborates the sap by its self, for it has chlorophyll carrying out its own photosynthesis process.

The **usnea** (12) or **barba de viejo** (old man's beard) is another vegetable which calls our attention for its abundance on tree trunks and branches. It is a lichen that is also found in the steppe, but it is specially abundant in the trees of this zone and the Magellanic forest.

Again on the nothofagus, once in a while a kind of knot that wraps branches or trunk can be seen: this is a defense reaction of the tree, that generates a hormonal hyperproduction (hiperplasia) due to the irritation produced by a parasitic fungus, the Cyttaria darwinii, that introduces itself in the tree through any hole (cuts, wounds). Its reproducing organs, a kind of yellowish balls, was called **pan de indio** (13) (Indian Bread), for the indians of the past nourished from it. They usually appear in Autumn or Winter.

Under the forest, other bushes like the **chaura** (14), with small apple looking berries and the **sietecamisas** (15), start to show up, **anemonas** (16) are abundant in Spring.

# MAGELLANIC FOREST

After you cross the National Park threshold, the ñires disappear, to leave space for another larger tree with straighter branches: the **lenga** (17). It is the most important and numerous tree of the zone, its size notoriously increases as we go westward. The lenga also delimits the upper parts of the forest, taking the shape of creeping bushes, at about 1000 m.a.s.l. but as we have mentioned before, this height varies in other Patagonian regions: In Lanin National Park, at 1800 m and in Tierra del Fuego, at only 600 m.

As we go on, another shrub attracts our attention, specially in Spring and beginning of Summer, when it fills of beautiful red flowers: the **notro** (18) also called **ciruelillo**. Though here it will always take the shape of an average size shrub, in other places it may become a small tree.

At ground level the **arvejillas** (19) are abundant, sometimes making big violet spots under the forest.

Always westward, about 7 km before reaching the glacier, some very special green trees start to appear, first very scarcely and then more frequently: they are the **guindos or coihues de magallanes** (20), they are the third Nothofagus of the zone and the only one with evergreen leaves. The coihue only grows in very damp zones, (over 800 mm annual rainfall) and can reach 25/30 m height. Near the Perito Moreno Glacier Division of the National Park, some beautiful specimens of this tree can be admired.

At that same place, some **canelos** (21) can be found. They are the Araucano's sacred trees and their bark has medicinal properties. In Tierra del Fuego, sailors used their leaves to cure scurvy.

Another damp zone tree is the **ciprés de las guaitecas** (22), it is an evergreen and only very few specimens can be found in the most western parts of the Park. In Chile it is also called "Ciprés de Mallín" for it can grow in the dampest parts of the ground. Its wood is almost nonputrescible, reason why it is almost extinct in the region, specially due to indiscriminated cuttings. The creation of the National Park in 1937, saved the last existing specimens.

The **leña dura** (23) is another tree that has also almost disappeared, but this time because of the cattle that once grazed in today's National Park, it is a shrub / tree of persistant foliage.

Other flowers and shrubs appear in the underforest in this zone: the **fucsia magallánica** o **chilco** (24), the **ourisia** (25), both in very shady and damp places, the **parrilla** (26), whose fruit is used to make marmalades, the **violet** (27), that is very abundant all about the Nothofagus underforest, the **mutilla** (28) a creeping and spread out shrub, that has red edible fruits. Its presence is a symptom of very low temperature, that is why together with the lenga, it is one of the last vegetables to be found in the highest zones.

In the Patagonia forest, from the most driest to the dampest zone, you can find 5 kinds of orchideas, the most common ones are the **orquidea amarilla** (29), that can be seen from the footpaths at the perito Moreno Glacier Front, and the **orquidea blanca**, or **palomita** (30) in shadier places, also near the Glacier.

Lastly, and before ending this chapter on Patagonian flora, we would like to quote two trees, that though they are not original of the zone, due to their strength, fast growth and adaptability, were adopted by all the estancias to make the protecting barriers against the wind: they are the **poplar** and the **willow**. They are the only traces of green in the midst of such a desolated landscape and they are the sure announcer of human presence in the Patagonian desert.

| COMMON NAME | SCIENTIFIC NAME | FAMILY |
|---|---|---|
| 1 Coirón | *Festuca gracilima* | Gramineous |
| 2 Calafate | *Berberis buxifolia* | Berberidaceas |
| | *Berberis heterophila* | |
| 3 Mata Negra | *Verbena tridens* | Compound |
| 4 Neneo | *Mulinum pinosum* | Umbelliferous |
| 5 Mata guanaco | *Anartrophilum rigidum* | Leguminous |
| 6 Paramela | *Adesmia boronoides* | Leguminous |
| 7 Romerillo | *Chiliotrichium rosmarinifolium* | Compound |
| 8 Zapatito de la virgen | *Calceolaria uniflora* | Crophulariaceous |
| 9 Topa topa | *Calceolaria biflora* | Scrophulariaceous |
| 10 Ñire | *Nothofagus antartica* | Fagaceous |
| 11 Farolillo chino | *Mizodendrum punctulatum* | Michodendraceous |
| 12 Barba de viejo | *Usnea usnea* | Usneaceous |
| 13 Pan de indio | *Cyttaria darwinii* | Cytaradialeous |
| 14 Chaura | *Pernttya mucronata* | Ericaceous |
| 15 Sietecamisas | *Escallonia rubra* | Saxifragaceous |
| 16 Anemonas | *Anemone multifida* | Ranunculaceous |
| 17 Lenga | *Nothofagus pumilio* | Fagaceous |
| 18 Notro | *Embotrium coccineum* | Proteaceous |
| 19 Arvejilla | *Lathyrus magellanicus* | Leguminous |
| 20 Guindo | *Nothofagus betuloides* | Fagaceous |
| 21 Ciprés de las guaitecas | *Pilgerodendrum uviferum* | Cupresaceous |
| 22 Leña dura | *Maytenus magellanica* | Celastraceous |
| 23 Canelo | *Drimys winteri* | Winteraceous |
| 24 Chilco | *Fuchsia magellanica* | Enoteraceous |
| 25 Ourisia | *Ourisia alpina* | Scrophulariaceous |
| 26 Parrilla | *Ribes magellanicum* | Saxifragaceous |
| 27 Violeta | *Viola maculata* | Violaceous |
| 28 Mutilla | *Empetrum rubrum* | Empetraceous |
| 29 Orquídea amarilla | *Gavilea lutea* | Orchidaceous |
| 30 Palomita | *Codonorchis lessonii* | Orchidaceous |

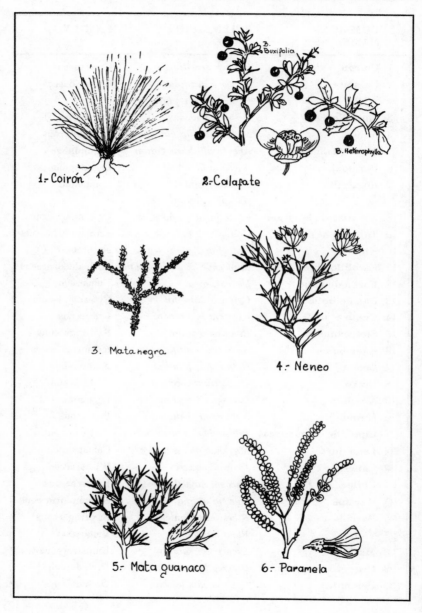

1.- Coirón

2.- Calafate

B. Buxifolia

B. Heterophylla

3. Mata negra

4.- Neneo

5.- Mata guanaco

6.- Paramela

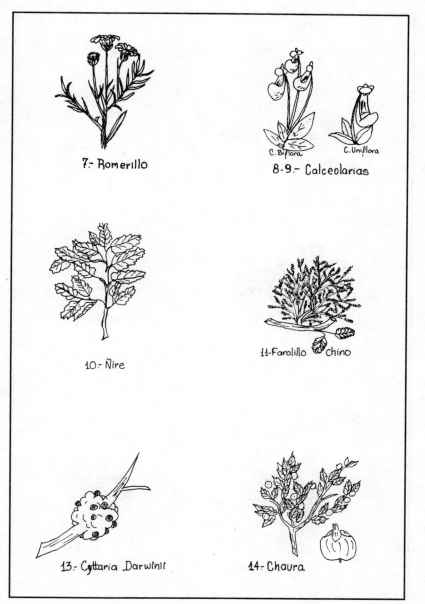

7.- Romerillo

8-9.- Calceolarias

C. Biflora    C. Uniflora

10.- Ñire

11-Farolillo Chino

13.- Cyttaria Darwinii

14- Chaura

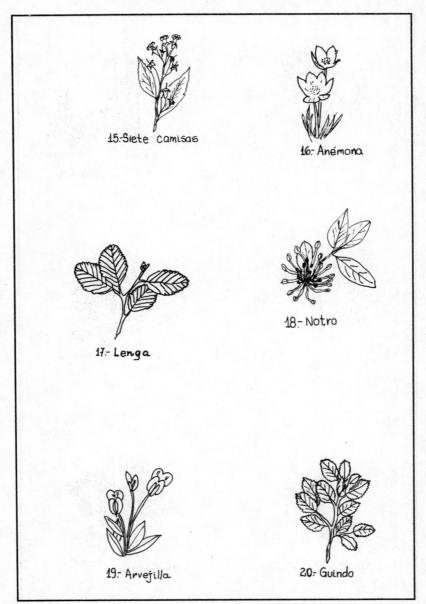

15.- Siete camisas

16.- Anémona

17.- Lenga

18.- Notro

19.- Arvejilla

20.- Guindo

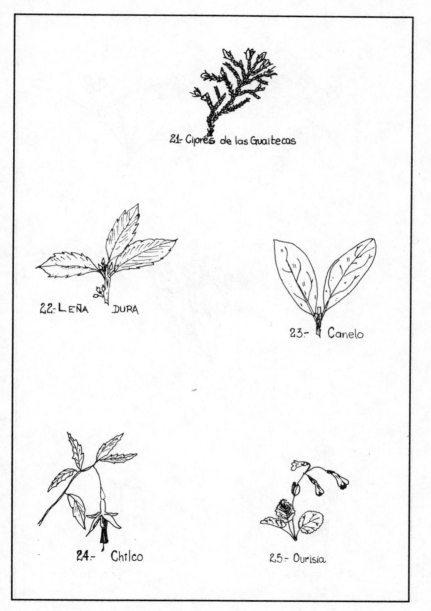

21.- Ciprés de las Guaitecas

22.- LEÑA DURA

23.- Canelo

24.- Chilco

25.- Ourisia

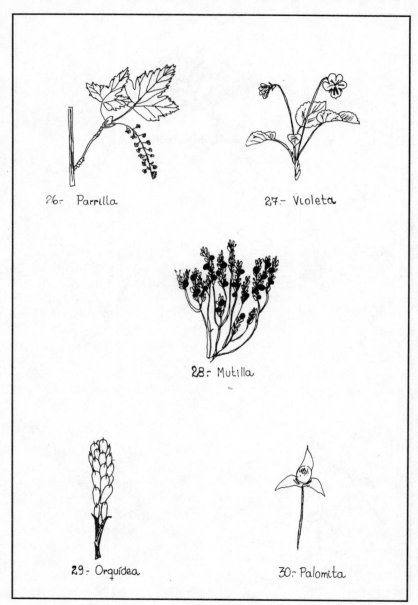

26.- Parrilla

27.- Violeta

28.- Mutilla

29.- Orquídea

30.- Palomita

# FAUNA

The following is a short list of mammals and fowls of the zone with their principal features. We have chosen them, because they are the ones that best represent or are most visible to the visitors to our region. Though not all have been included, we hope the ones that have been are interesting to all.

## MAMMALS

### PUMA
*Felis concolor patagonica*

**Order:** Carnivorous

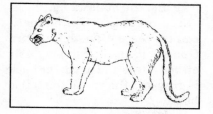

**Family:** Felidae
**Size:**
Up to 3 meters long, from the snout to the end of the tail and can weigh between 50 and 80 kg.
**Feeding:**
It is diverse: from fowls such as upland geese or lesser rheas to large mammals like the guanacos, fox and of course, sheep and lambs.
**Reproduction:**
It can have as many as 6 cubs, but the most usual are 3 or 4.
**Predators:**
It has no natural predator. They are hunted pitilessly due to the great losses they produce among the flocks. In the old days, when the estancias were more populated, there was a "leonero" in each one (In Patagonia the puma is called "el león" (the lion) whose

job was to hunt it. The ideal time is the end of Autumn, when the first snows make its tracks easy to follow by the dogs that are specially trained for this purpose. Still today, the estancia owners, pay the death of an animal at sight of the skin, that on the other hand has no commercial value.

**Habits:**

It is an animal of night habits. It lives near the Cordillera and in the steppe zone, near cliffs or rock formations, that are their shelter during the daytime. It is a great walker, it can walk over 40 km a night. Its hunting territories are enormous (from 40 to 60 km$^2$) and it frequently marks them with small piles of leaves, on which it repeatedly urinates. As many feline animals, it is not very fast at racing, except for the first meters, that is why its hunting techniques consist of getting as close as possible to his prey, leap suddenly on its back and bend its neck backward, in the case of big animals like guanacos or colts. The puma is most dangerous to the flock when the mother is teaching the cubs how to hunt. It is a shy animal, completely harmless to man.

In the zone, there are two other kinds of wild cats, that also belong to the feline family:

the **cat of the grass fields** (Felis colocolo) and the **mountain cat** (Felis geoffroyi) that just like the fox we will now describe, they have the bad luck of having commercially valuable fur, and therefore they are persued and hunted, generally with traps that are set up all over the country. The produce from the selling of their furs, is again the second income for the estancia workers, even though the old story is again repeated, it is the intermediary who makes the most substantial profit.

## RED FOX
*Dusicyon culpaeus*

**Order:** Carnivorous
**Family:** Canidae (wolves, jackels...)

**Size, weight, aspect:**

Up to 1.30 m. long from snout to the end of the tail, that represents approximately one third of its length. A specimen of a subspecies from Tierra del Fuego, of 1.50 m long has been found. The female weighs about 9 kg and the male 12 kg.

It is the largest South American fox (except for the Aguará Guazú), it has redish long hair on belly, legs and head, the back is gray and the end of the tail is black.

**Feeding:**
Its main diet is based on eggs, fowls and rodents, though it may also feed on sheep, specially lambs.

**Reproduction:**
It can have up to 5 offsprings.

**Predators:**
Its only natural predator is the puma. Nevertheless, it is constantly hunted by the estancia owners and workers, due to its constant raids against the sheep and for its valuable skin.

**Comments:**
Even though it is true that the red fox is responsible for the death of many sheep and lambs (on some estancias up to 15 % annually of the stock) it seems all fox do not have the habit of killing sheep. The percentage depends on each estancia of its "ecologic health": the better the grass, herbs, etc to feed on birds and rodents, the less the fox will be in the need of killing sheep and lambs. On the other hand, the method that has been used up to now to eliminate it, specially strychnine, can be terri-

bly negative for the landowner due to the extinction of animals that feed on the dead fox: condors, eagles, caracaras, etc and leaves the environment unprotected of predators and carrion birds, that are indispensable for the ecologic balance for the country, in the long run.

## PATAGONIAN FOX
*Dusicyon griseus*

**Order:** Carnivorous
**Family:** Canidae

**Size, weight, aspect:**
It is about 80 to 90 cm long, 30 to 36 cm belong to the tail. It weighs between 3,5 and 4 kg. It is smaller than the latter, it is a grayish color, legs and flanks are slightly reddish and the end of the tail is dark.

**Feeding:**
Its diet includes all kinds of insects, rodents, fowls, eggs, hares and carrion, and berries like the calafate, chaura or zarzaparrilla.

**Reproduction:**
It can have up to 6 offsprings.

**Predators:**
Like the red fox, its natural predator is the puma. Its skin, though less commercially valuable than the latter, is used in the furrier business, therefore it is also a victim of the traps that are scattered all over the coun-

try. The constant persecution of both the red and gray fox, has consequently reduced its number, and has made the puma, now lacking its natural prey, become constantly fonder of sheep, thus producing the contrary effect that had been sought. This is something very frequent when the ecologic - feeding chain of an animal is broken.

**Comments:**
Lately, it is being displaced in the zone by the Red fox, which is more voracious and aggressive.

## GUANACO
### *Lama guanicoe*

**Order:** Artyodactila
**Family:** Camelidae (the other three members of the family in Latin America are the llama, the alpaca and the vicuña.
**Size, weight, aspect:**
It is the tallest of all the Argentine land fauna. It is about 1.10

m tall and the distance between its snout and the base of the tail is 1,85 m. It weighs between 120 and 150 kg. It looks like a llama, with longer legs and has the ocherish-cinnamon color of the vicuña. It has thick hair and long eye lashes. Its has well differenciated padded cloven hoofs.
**Feeding:**
Herbivorous, based on grass and occasionales bushes and lichens, specially in winter.
**Reproduction:**
It has an offspring per year, in Spring or Summer, after 11 months gestation. A few days after birth, the copulations for the next year are done.
**Predators:**
Its natural predator is the puma, though the offsprings or chulengos are persecuted by men on account of their fine fur, which they change at two months of age. The red fox is also an occasional predator specially of the chulengos.

## Comments:

The guanaco is found all along the Andes from Bolivia to Tierra del Fuego. It is a habitual inhabitant of the steppes, it is hardly ever seen in the forests, except in Tierra del Fuego, where it commonly seeks protection in Winter. Together with the ñandu or Lesser Rhea, it was the basis of subsistence for the past Tehuelches, whose indian camps and clothing were made out of guanaco skins.

It is a gregarious animal which forms groups of one male and several females. The male does not let other males approach his troop, he keeps a constant surveillance over his harem from aloft. Whenever there is the least evidence of danger, he lets out a kind of neigh, to let the rest of the group know it should run away.

Away from the breeding time, much larger groups are formed with hundreds of members. The males that do not have females, also form their own groups, and lastly the old males often wander alone.

They usually defecate in a common place, forming a great circle of dung, where the ñandúes come in search of insects. The "powder baths" are also frequent in their territory; they are places where the animals wallow in to clean their hair and free it from external parasites.

In Spring, when they are in heat, the males have violent fights and persecutions, where they spit each other in the face . This habit has made their relatives, the llamas and the alpacas famous.

They have a characteristic mange, that they do not transmit to sheep, as it is generally believed, and for which they are expelled from the group by the other members.

Contrarily to sheep, that due to their sharp hoofs and their way of grazing, often pull out the grass, thus provoking the cuasi desertification of great extensions of the steppe, the guanaco has padded hoofs, and when it feeds, it does not pull out the vegetaion but cuts it instead. Due to the latter, there are several experiments of breeding them in captivity in Patagonia, with excellent results till present. The higher quality of its wool, at a time when sheep wool price keeps on going down, in a market that is being increasingly dominated by synthetic fibers, the guanaco's wool has become a hope for the depressed Patagonian wool production.

## EUROPEAN HARE
*Lepus capensis*

**Order:** Lagomorpha
**Family:** Leporidae (rabbits)
**Size, weight, aspect:**
It can be up to 65 cm long and weigh 4 kg. Its brownish color is easily mistaken for the steppe colors.
**Feeding:** Herbivorous
**Reproduction:**
Contrarily to its rabbit relatives, that are very fertile, the hare has only one brood a year, of one or two offsprings.
**Predators:**
Pumas, fox and wild cats have been the natural predators since it was brought from Europe at the end of the XIX century. Lately, they are being hunted in the winter time, later canned and exported, principally to Europe.
**Comments:**
As we have said before, the hare hunt in the winter time, has been a more frequent activity in

the last years. During the night, vehicles with powerful turning lights, travel along the roads dazzling the animals and shooting them. On a good night, a vehicle can "harvest" over 150. In the Argentino Lake area alone, about 30,000 animals a year have been hunt during the past seasons.

## SKUNK
*Conepatus humboldtii*

**Order:** Carnivorous
**Family:** Mustilelidae (ferrets, weasels, rive wolves...)
**Size, weight, aspect:**
50 to 60 cm full length, the tail is about one third. Of an ocherish brown color with two white stripes from the snout to the tail.
**Feeding:**
Omnivorous, for it eats from insects and rodents to fruits and roots.
**Reproduction:**
After a month and a half gestation, it can have up to 3 to 4 offsprings in Spring.
**Predators:**
The Patagonian carnivorous animals (pumas, fox, mountain cats) are their natural predators, though they have the bad luck of having a commercially valuable skin, so, as it is natural, they are

decimated, by the rural people. It is often caught in the traps that were set up for the fox.

from roots to fowl eggs, that he reaches by boring tunnels under the nests.

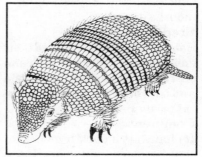

**Predators:**
Its natural predators are the Patagonian carnivorous animals (pumas, fox ...)

**Comments:**
It defends itself from its predators with a highly unpleasant smelling liquid, that with great aim it shoots from the base of its tail, up to 4 meters distance. The pestilent liquid can be very urticating in contact with eyes, though it will not blind, as it is generally believed.

They can be very docile pets in captivity, but of course after eliminating the secretory gland.

**Comments:**
They belong to the same family as the High Andes armadillo, but its shell is not used in Patagonia to make instruments (charangos). Its meat is a treat for the country man. It is shy and slow, it can only protect itself by rapidly digging up a hole and burying himself in it, when it senses any kind of danger, or hiding itself completely inside its shell.

### ARMADILLO
*Z  rerius pichyi-pichyi*

**Order:** Xenarthra
**Family:** Dasypodidae
**Size and weight:**
Up to 40 cm and 3 kg.
**Feeding:**
Omnivorous. Its diet includes

### HUEMUL
*Hipocamellus bisulcus*

**Order:** Artyodactila
**Family:** Cervidae
**Size and weight:**
At the cross it can reach 80 cm

length and weigh up to 100 kg.
**Feeding:** Herbivorous
**Reproduction:**
One offspring a year. 6 to 7 months gestation.
**Predators:**
Before the arrival of men to their environs (cordillera forests and surrounding steppes) the puma and the red fox were their natural predators.
**Comments:**
Its hair has a dark brown color that becomes lighter in winter. The males have small antlers that they change annually. They are hardly seen in the zone. Today they are almost extinct, though in the past there were a great number of them. The few that remain, hide in the most inaccessible canyons of the Cordillera. They were eliminated because of their tameness and trust. Regarding this last comment, we quote some paragraphs from Andreas Madsen's memories, a Danish pioneer of the

pioneers of the Chalten zone: "When I close my eyes and go back into the past, I am sad and weary to recall yesterday's forests full of deer peacefully grazing". The large wool companies start to settle in the region, Madsen tells us about their methods: "When they arrived with their machinery to cut wood in the forest to make buildings, and fence posts, they did not only cut what they needed but they burnt and destroyed the rest only for the fun of it. They made big killings, by the dozen at the time, to try out their weapons, leaving the bodies to rot".

# FOWLS

In the Lake Argentino zone, due to the very diverse ecosystem, (cordillera, steppe, lake, shallow coastal lagunas, etc.) almost all the Patagonian fowls can be found, except of course the marine ones. The purpose of this paper is not to list them but to comment on the most frequent and visble to our visitors.

**ANDEAN CONDOR**
*Vultur griphus*

**Order:** Falconiform
**Family:** Cathartidae

**Size:**
The largest American bird, it can have up to a 3m wingspan.
**Feeding:**
It mostly feeds on carrion, though when it is in need, it can hunt small offsprings abandoned by their mothers.
**Reproduction:**
It lays only one egg. The offspring takes 3 years to become an adult.
**Habits:**
It is the symbol and emperor of the Andes. It lives in the mountains. It nests in the high rocks, never in trees, and its perfect gliding, allows it to go as far up as 10000 m high, though in our zone it often flies much lower. Its eyesight is eight times more acute than human, which allows it to cover an enormous surveillance radius seeking for food, when in the air.

The adults differ from the young by a white feather collar and the female from the male, by the crest and flesh on the collar of the latter. Except when it comes down to eat, it is never seen resting on the ground, because due to its wingspan, it has a hard time taking off. It always rests on vertical cliffs. It is an excellent glider, and only in total absence of wind, does it flutter.

## BLACK CHESTED BUZZARD EAGLE
*Geranoetus melanoleucus*

**Order:** Falconiform
**Family:** Accipitridae
**Size:**
65 cm the male and the female a little larger.
**Feeding:**
Dead animals, small mammals and fowls. It often eats carrion, while the rest of the possible eaters, (caranchos, chimangos) patiently wait for their turn. It also feeds on small newly born lambs that separate from their mothers.
**Reproduction:**
It lays 1 or 2 eggs. The young have brown feathers, with brownish cinnamon spots. Like most of its order, it takes years to get its definite feathers, that is a light gray color with a white chest and black around the head.
**Habits:**
It slowly glides at great heights, for which it is often mistaken for

a condor, and which it is differenciated from by its triangular wings.

It usually nests on the cliff tops, from where he can look out on his hunting territory, and sometimes on the tree tops. It only cries out near its nest, and the sound resembles a wild human laugh.

## CRESTED CARACARA
*Polyborus plancus*

**Order:** Falconiform
**Family:** Falconidae
**Size:** About 60 cm
**Feeding:**
Eats anything. From carrion to live prey, including lambs and sick sheep.
**Reproduction:** From 2 to 3 eggs.
**Habits:**
It is spread all over South America. Due to its slyness and

resources, it is included in the mythology of many Precolombian people, from the Incas to the Tierra del Fuego Onas. Even today, it is still found all over: Inhospitable or populated areas, steppes or forests. It is daring and quarrelsome, and when the males fight in the periods they are in heat, more than one dies, and is quickly eaten up by the rest. They form live lasting couples and they also rest at fixed places, if it should be a tree, on the same branch.

There is no difference between the male and female's feathers. The young are a dirty creamy color, that is a little darker toward the head.

## CHIMANGO CARACARA
*Milvago chimango*

**Order:** Falconiform
**Family:** Falconidae
**Size:** From 37 to 40 cm.

**Feeding:**
Like the crested caracara, it has a diverse diet, and will also attack lambs separated from their mothers.
**Reproduction:**
From 2 to 3 eggs.
**Habits:**
Like the carancho, it dwells all over, eating specially carrion, for which, even though it should sometimes kill a lamb, it is very useful in the country, for it eliminates a number of insects, rodents and rotten matter, that can transmit deseases.

### AMERICAN KESTREL
*Falco spaverius*

**Order:** Falconiform
**Family:** Falconidae
**Size:** 25 cm the male and 28 the female.
**Feeding:** Small rodents.

### LESSER RHEA
*Pterocnemia pennata*

**Order:** Rheiform
**Family:** Rheidae
**Size:** The males up to 1 meter.

**Feeding:**
Herbs and insects. In captivity, it is liable of swallow anything, from meat to coins.

**Reproduction:**
Polygamous, all the females of the group lay the eggs in the same nest, that has been previously built by the male. The male does the incubation that lasts about 40 days, hardly getting up from the nest. Once the pigeons are born, also called charos, up to 40 can be born, it is still the father that looks after them.

**Comments:**
It is a typical steppe inhabitant, its feathers and meat were always coveted by the Tehuelches. Though it resembles an ostrich, it has some differences with the Australian or African ostrich; for example it has two fingers instead of three.

It is very distrustful and difficult to aproach, and the best way to protect itself is by running away. It can reach speeds up to 45 km an hour. Nevertheless, to protect its progeny, it will face any man or animal that might threaten them.

It is very easy to domesticate, and it will follow its master like a dog.

### SOUTHERN LAPWING
*Vanellus chilensis*

**Order:** Charadriiform
**Family:** Charadriidae

**Size:** 35 cm
**Feeding:** Insects, caterpillar, larvae, worms...
**Reproduction:**
From 2 to 3 eggs.
**Comments:**
It is one of the most well known and distributed birds in the country. It migrates to our zone and its arrival announces Spring. It is always very aggressive, but specially when it comes to defending its nest. It attacks in short and acrobatic flights any human or animal that approaches its territory, making a high pitched cry . Not even eagles can fly near their domains without being furiously attacked by. On the estancias, it is the perfect guardian, for it announces a strange presence, even before dogs do, and attacks it making a great noise.

## BUFF NECKED IBIS
### *Theristicus Caudatus*

**Order:** Ardeiform
**Family:** Threskiornithidae
**Size:** 60 cm
**Feeding:**
Herbs, worms and insects.
**Reproduction:**
It nests in the rush and near lagunas. It lays 2 to 3 eggs.

**Reproduction:**
From 5 to 8 eggs.
**Comments:**
It always lives near damp places. It forms a life time couple. At the end of Autumn it concentrates in large flocks and flies north. The male is white and black and the female brown with black stipes.

**Comments:**
It belongs to the ibis family, and it makes a characteristic nasal sound like a horn. It always lives near damp places and it goes north in the winter. It often flies very high letting out its horn cry.

## UPLAND GOOSE
### *Cloephaga picta*

**Order:** Anseriform
**Family:** Anatidae
**Size:** 75 cm
**Feeding:** Green grass

## BLACK NECKED SWAM
### *Cygnus melancoryphus*

**Order:** Anseriform
**Family:** Anatidae
**Size:** 120 cm
**Feeding:**
Aquatic plants, insects, and in the sea, mollusks.
**Reproduction:**
It lays 5 to 7 eggs.
**Comments:**
There are no morphological differences between male and fe male. Like the upland goose they

**Feeding:**
Aquatic insects, small mollusks..
**Reproduction:**
An egg, seldom two.
**Comments:**
Of the three species that dwell in Latin America, this is the only one in our zone. It always lives in places with abundant and shallow water, and though it swims, due to its long legs it rather walks. To eat, it puts its beak up side down, that is, the top part on the bottom of the water, and with a fast and continuous movement of the tongue, it inhales and expels water, trapping between the corneous laminas of its beak, sea weeds and crustaceans, that it feeds on and whose pigments, are responsible

also have a life time mate. They live in aquatic surroundings, even sea coasts. It has a difficult take off, but once in the air, it is fast and powerful, and it makes a loud fluttering sound. It is distrustful of human approach, because it has been persecuted for its beautiful feathers (Tales of the past century, tell that the gauchos in Central Argentina would make wooden boleadoras to hunt them; if they missed the shot, the weapon would remain floating in the water). In case of danger, the offsprings get on their parents back, to make a faster escape.

It migrates in winter.

### CHILEAN FLAMINGO
*Phoenicopterus chilensis*

**Order:** Phoenicopteriform
**Family:** Phoenicopteridae
**Size:** 1 meter, the female is a little smaller.

Flamencos° - *Phoenicopterus chilensis*

Ostrero austral - *Haematopus leucopodus*

Pato de los torrentes - *Merganetta armata*

Cisne de cuello negro - *Cygnus melancoryphus*

Coscoroba - *Coscoroba coscoroba*

Fitz Roy - Chaltén

for the characteristic color of its feathers. When feathers fall, they lose the color rapidly. When these animals are in captivity, as in zoos for example, they are fed carrots or red peppers, to give them their beautiful color. They are good fliers, and in winter they migrate northward.

There is no difference between male and female. The young are mostly a whitish color.

## MAGELLANIC OYSTERCATCHER
*Haematopus leucopodus*

**Order:** Charadriiform
**Family:** Haematopudidae
**Size:** 40 cm
**Feeding:**
Larvae, insects, crustacean...
**Reproduction:**
From 2 to 3 eggs.
**Comments:**
Its favorite environs are the sea coasts, though it often visits water courses and inner lagunas (ponds), specially in summer. It is very nervous and agitated. It can be easily recognized by the high pitched cry it makes.

Its name is due to the fact that, when it gets to the oyster banks, it introduces its long and flattened beak between the half open shells of the mollusks, it cuts the muscles that close the shell, and then it calmly eats the animal up.

There is no difference between the two sexes' feathers.

## LONG TAILED MEADOWLARK
*Sturnella loyca*

**Order:** Passeriform

**Family:** Icteridae
**Size:** 22 cm
**Feeding:**
Insects,worms, seeds...
**Reproduction:**
It nests on the ground. It lays from 3 to 4 eggs.
**Comments:**
It is easily identified, for the bright red color of its breast and continuous singing, even on winter days, because it lives in the zone all year round. In this season it forms large flocks.

It has land habits. it hides its nest at the base of a bush, where it never arrives at flying; he lands at a certain distance, and then walks up to the hiding place.

The female is a little smaller than the male, and her colors are less brighter than his.

### ROFOUS BACKED NEGRITO
*Lessonia rufa*

**Order:** Passeriform
**Family:** Tyranidae
**Size:** 11 cm
**Reproduction:**
From 3 to 4 eggs
**Comments:**
Great difference between sexes: The male is black with a brownish reddish back and the female is coffee color.

It is restless and active, with a swift flight and land habits, it migrates northward in winter.

### RUFOUS COLLARED SPARROW
*Zornotrichia capensis*

**Order:** Passeriform
**Family:** Emberizidae
**Size:** 14 cm
**Reproduction:** 3 to 5 eggs
**Feeding:**
Seeds, grain, larvae, insects... It hunts the latter by the score when feeding its off springs, that

like all new born fowls, are insectivorous.

**Comments:**

It is the most common fowl in the country that could not be absent in the region. It is very restless and daring, it can be found everywhere, from the forests to the Cordillera even in the steppe. It wanders in the outskirts of towns and cities like the sparrow.

It has a slight sexual dimorfism: The male has brighter colors and a small crest.

**Size:** 35 cm

**Reproduction:**

Its favorite nests are tree holes, where it lays 4 to 6 eggs.

**Feeding:** Grain and seeds.

**Comments:**

It is the most southern of all the family, it usually lives in great flocks that are easily located for the continuous riot they make. It is generally found in the forest, though it migrates in winter, or goes out into more open spaces.

## AUSTRAL PARAKEET
*Enicognatus ferrugineus*

**Order:** Psittaciform
**Family:** Psittacidae

## MAGELLANIC WOODPECKER
*Campephilus magellanicus*

**Order:** Piciform
**Family:** Picidae
**Size:** 40 cm
**Feeding:**
It mainly feeds on larvae that it traps, after boring the tree trunks with its stong pecking.
**Reproduction:** Like the latter, it also lays its eggs in tree holes, where it lays 3 to 5 eggs.
**Comments:**
Undoubtedly, its the most beautiful bird in our forest. It can usually be seen flying from one tree to another. The dry sound of its pecking, makes it easily identifiable, and it is easy to approach, for it is quite trusting. It is permanently seeking for larvae, and can climb up to the very tree top.

The male has a red head and a black body, while the female is completey black, with white feathers on the back and a more pointed crest.

---

To end this brief chapter on the local fauna, I would like to recommend a visit to **Laguna Nimes** in the surroundings of **Calafate** (see map in this same book): only a 15 minute walk from downtown, next to Argentino Lake. Many of the species mentioned above live in this small laguna and surroundings (flamingos, upland geese, swans, chimangos, caracaras...) besides, there is a great variety of ducks, grebes and widgeons: the following are some that can be found there.

| | |
|---|---|
| **Brown pintail** | *Anas georgica* |
| **Southern widgeon** | *Anas sibilatrix* |
| **Red Shoveler** | *Anas platalea* |
| **Crested duck** | *Lophonetta specularoides* |
| **Spectacled duck** | *Anas specularis* |
| **Speckled teal** | *Anas flavirostris* |
| **Flying streamer duck** | *Tachyeres patachonicus* |
| **Andean ruddy duck** | *Oxyura ferruginea* |
| **White tufted grebe** | *Podiceps rolland* |
| **Silvery grebe** | *Podiceps occipitalis* |
| **White winged coot** | *Fulica leucoptera* |
| **Red gartered coot** | *Fulica armillata* |

# PATAGONIAN MARINE FAUNA[1]

The Patagonian marine fauna can be divided into two large groups: fowls (penguins, cormorants) and mammals. The latter, can be subdivided into pinnipeds (seals and sea lions) and cetaceans (whales and dolphins). Both the cetaceans and pinnipeds are land mammals that have developed a great adaptation to water, adopting hydrodynamic shapes, turning their limbs into fins and retracting external organs. Nevertheless, they all breathe by means of lungs, and therefore have to surface on a regular basis, and regarding the pinnipeds, they return to land to carry out their reproductive and breeding cycles.

## COMMERSON'S DOLPHIN
*Cephalorhynchus commersonii*

**Order**: Cetaceous
**Family**: Delphindae
**Size**: Males: 1,45 m.
Females: 1,50 m.
**Weight**: About 40 kg.

It frequents all the Patagonian coast, Magellan Straits, Tierra del Fuego and Chilean Austral Islands. Occasionally, it will go up rivers and estuaries.

They have unmistakable contrasting black and white colors and can be seen in rather large groups of approximately 5 to 10 individuals. They are curious and bold. They frequently approach ships, and sometimes swim along side the prow, with

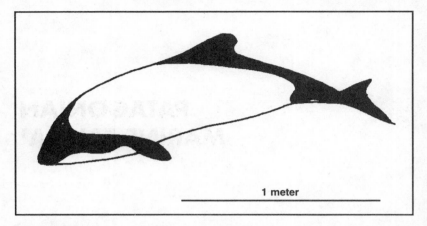

1 meter

their bellies upwards. They can also be seen from shore, due to one of their hunting techniques: they surround their prey (small fish and squids) against the coast in shallow waters, or take advantage of the large tides of the zone to intercept them during the low tide.

They are frequently hunted by fishermen, who use their meat as bait for center fish traps. The also die, when they incidentally fall in the nets for haddocks and crawfish.

### ORCA
*Orcinus orca*

**Order**: Cetaceous
**Family**: Delphindae
**Size**: Males: 9,5 m -
Females: 7,5 m
**Weight**: Males: 8000 kg
Females: 4000 kg

The orca is better known as the killer whale and it is one of the most extended marine mammals, from the Ecuador to the Poles.

Their contrasting black and white color and large dorsal fin, which can be up to 1,80 m long, make them easy to recognize. These same characters allow us to individualize each member of the species; for both the spots, as well as certain characteristic shapes of the fin, are particular and different on each animal. Regarding the latter, it is smaller and more curved on the females and the young, than on the males.

10 to 12 large pairs of teeth, a great strength in the water and a developed intelligence, make the orca, one of the great marine predators. Its gestation period

lasts 15 months, and females can live up to 80 years and males up to 60, though the average life span is reduced to half that period for both sexes.

Their behavior and organization has been studied on the west Canadian coast (British Columbia, Vancouver Island) since 1973. We have sumarized the following data from these observations: The orcas gather into two kinds of groups, which have very different habits. One of the groups, called in the scientific jargon "residents", form large stable groups, to the point of integrating, up to 3 and 4 generations of individuals within them, which is rather exceptional in the animal kingdom. They are sedentary in the said zone. They feed on salmons (herrings, in the case of Norwegian orcas), and they accompany the schools of said fish during their migrations. But perhaps the most amazing feature of these groups, is the variety of sounds they make: an enormous acoustic repertoire constantly communicates the members of the same group and helps to keep them together in zones of poor visibility, as well as allows them to interchange informa-

1 meter

tion about fishing zones...etc.. What is really unique about these sounds, is that they have their own characteristics for each group, which have developed into real"dialects"that allow the unity of the group when it gets mixed up with others, maybe to enable crossing and thus avoiding the endogamy.

The second group is formed by orcas called"transients". Not only are these groups much smaller than those of the residents and their displacements more erratic, but they are also more limited in their sounds. The main difference with the others, is their diet: while the residents feed on fish, ignoring the abundant marine mammal colonies in the zone, the transients have precisely specialized on hunting said animals (sea lions and seals), traveling long distances to do so.

The two groups mentioned above, carefully avoid encountering each other in the same waters.

In Argentina, you can often see groups of orcas, specially during the autumn at Valdés Peninsula, where they are currently studied. These orcas, are more related to the group of transients of the northern hemisphere, and therefore they are

marine mammal hunters. Their presence in autumn, is due to the fact, that at that time, the young sea lions and elephant seals, start adventuring into the water and their inexperience, make them an easy prey for their sly predators. The hunting technique is as daring as it is spectacular: at a certain distance from the shore, the members of the group line up, thus preventing the the sea lions from escaping toward deeper waters. One of the members (sometimes two, while the mother teaches her cub) approaches the prey, which is swimming and splashing carefreely, near the shore. In the midst of an enormous uproar of foam, the orca emerges from the water, traps its prey between its huge jaws, grounding itself almost completely on the shore of rolling stones. With powerful contortions and blows of the tail, the orca returns to the water with the prey between its teeth where the rest of the members of the group await their share of the loot.

Also at North End of Valdés Peninsula, once a right whale (perhaps old or ill) was attacked and eventually killed by several orcas.

Due to its intelligence and spectacularity, the orca has

lately become one of the principal attractions in many aquariums throughout the world.

## MAGELLAN PENGUINS
*Spheniscus magellanicus*

**Order**: Spenisciforme
**Family**: Spheniscidae
**Size**: 44 cm. (The males are slightly larger than the females)
**Weight**: About 4 kg.

Another of the great fauna attractions of the region, and one of the symbols of the extreme south of the globe, is the Magellan Penguin. It owes its name to Pigafetta, Magellan's chronicler, who on his first trip around the world, referred to it as"a kind of strange goose"The other name of"dumb bird"by which it was also known for a long time, was due to its clumsiness to move on land. Contrarily in the water, it moves around with great agility and swiftness. Its scientific name "Spheniscus" means "with the shape of a wedge", that properly describes its posture and way of diving.

Of the 18 species of penguins that are currently known, this one is by far the most abundant on the Patagonian coast, forming numerous reproduction colonies along the coastline (Camarones, Puerto Deseado, Monte León, Cabo Vírgenes, Canal de Beagle...). The most im-

1 meter

portant of all, is Punta Tombo in the Province of Chubut, where every year from September to March, about 225.000 couples gather, which added up to their respective offspring's (two per couple) reach almost a million individuals, at the peak of the breeding period, constituting the largest continental colony of the species out of Antarctica.

The males start arriving in the month of September to occupy the same nests they left the year before, which are sometimes located up to 800m from the coast. Though the largest concentration of nests, as is logical, is near the water and among the roots of large shrubs that hide them and protect them from the predators. Some days later, the first females arrive and together with them the eternal conflict of all the species: the first struggles among the males. Even though the penguin is a monogamous animal and forms stable families, the 4/5 year old males, that have just reached sexual maturity, will seek a female and a nest by means of struggles, where sometimes one of the contenders is killed.

The females lay 2 eggs in October, and after approximately 40 days of incubation, in November, the first pigeons, cov-

ered with grayish feathers, are born. From then on, the parents double their vigilance: gulls and skuas now join the list of the former predators (foxes, skunks, armadillos...), they continuously fly over the colony to hunt the pigeons. The latter are carefully kept in the bottom of the nest, and while one of the parents seeks food at sea, the other remains on guard at the nest. Generally, only one of the the two offspring's survives, and depending on the years, the reproductive success only reaches one percent of the eggs. During the years of scarce food, it is quite normal that the female abandons the nest to seek food at sea, leaving her young ones at the mercy of the predators mentioned before, since she is not relieved on time by her partner, that must wander great distances to obtain the pittance.

Once in the water, their natural predators are the orcas, the seals, and the giant petrel. Another cause of this species mortality, which has unfortunately become increasingly more common, is the petrolment they suffer due to the oil spills: the penguin's plumage becomes waterproof by the secretion of its skin which isolates it and allows it to survive in cold waters. When this protection is annulled by the petroleum, the animal is obliged to go on shore, where a slow agony awaits it due to cold and hunger.

It mainly feeds on anchovy, sardine, mackerel and squid, that they trap during short dives, (approximately 1 minute duration) where they can develop great swimming speed in truely underwater flights, where the fins work as propellers and the tail as a rudder.

In February, the young have already changed their first feathers for a juvenile plumage. They begin their first swimming and grooming lessons, especially during the morning and afternoon, when the heat is not too intense. The beach becomes populated by the youngsters, that thanks to their continuous pecking, keep their plumage in perfect shape or they rehearse new pirouettes in the water.

Towards March, the colony starts to abandon their nests to live another six months in the water, where they even sleep. They swim in large groups, at an average speed of 8 km/h and are bound for places as far as southern Brazil (penguins from Punta Tombo have been found off the shore of Rio de Janeiro) or Antarctica.

# SOUTH AMERICAN SEA LION
## *Otaria flavescens*

**Order**: Pinnipedia
**Family**: Otariidae
**Size**: 2,30 m/ 1,80 m
(males /females)
**Weight**: 300 kg / 150 kg
(males /females)

They are known as sea lions, due to the male's beautiful mane. They belong to the family of the otarides, whose principal differences with the focides (elephant seals), are the visible ears and the way they move their lower limbs on land, like the quadruped. They are called "one haired"to differentiate them from the fine sea lion or "two haired"(Arctocephalus australis) which has two different kinds of hairs on its skin, a fact which provoked its almost complete extinction due to its coveted value in the fur industry.

It can be found along all the Patagonian coast, though the places that are most accessible and therefore most visited, are Punta Piramides (Valdés Peninsula) and the Island of the Lions (Beagle Channel). On this island, it lives together with the two haired sea lion, though their reproductive periods are different.

It feeds on fish, squid and some crustaceans, and its natural predator are the orcas. In southern latitudes (Buenos Aires Province, Uruguay) they are also hunted by shark. As a result of some researches, regarding their feeding habits, it is concluded that they are mostly night feeders and on dark nights, (new moon and crescent): this is due to the fact that its prey are obliged, because of the dim light, to come up closer to the surface.

The females are sexually mature at 4/5 years, and from then on, during the breeding period, they annually use the same breeding stations. Taking into account that the offspring's can swim only after 15 days of birth, the stations are generally protected places and with an easy access to water. The males are the first to arrive, followed by the females a few days later. On arrival, each male forms its harem, that can reach up to a dozen females, though generally it does not surpass 5 or 6. From there on, the male's main and most exhausting task will be to defend the females from the harassment of the other males. All means are good to keep away competition: defying grunts, upright positions where it spreads out its bulky mane, and if there is no other way out, there will be a fight, that though very bloody, it is never mortal: the loser will prudently back up and try luck elsewhere.

Births take place in January and copulation approximately a week after the delivery, during the only two days of heat that the female annually has. The gestation lasts a year. The offspring's are black at birth, about 80 cm long and weigh 12 kg. Their milk feeding period is very long (six to ten months)

Like other species of otarides and focides, stones and pebbles are frequently found in their stomachs. Naturalists have given many explanations to this this fact : to facilitate digestion, -like in the case of certain fowls-, to balance diving, to avoid proliferation of parasites in the digestive system, to avoid hunger during the fasting periods, principally during the reproduction phase, when the animal must remain on land during long periods...

Due to different archaeological studies, we know that the Patagonia indians (Tehuelches, Onas, Yaganes and alacalufes) benefited from the sea lions to obtain food and to manufacture utensils: defenseless on land, curious in the water, punctual and predictable at their breeding stations, abundant in meat and lard, -that are so necessary in these climates-, the pinnipeds were always an easy prey for the aborigines. The hunting techniques would vary according to the places: approaching the beach during low tide cutting off and preventing their escape towards the sea, and then beating them up to death, was the method of the Tehuelches of the steppes; harpooning them with harpoons made out of guanaco bones from canoes, as the Yaganes in the Beagle channel used to hunt them. Other elements such as leather nets, bows and arrows and even throwing trunks and stones down from the cliffs at them, were used.

Six thousand years of this relationship does not seem to have deeply affected the survival of the prey: it will be the arrival of the white man, with his sacred banners of progress and short run benefit who will end with it all. We have already seen some facts about the disappearance of the aborigines and now we will see a little about the disappearance of the sea lions:

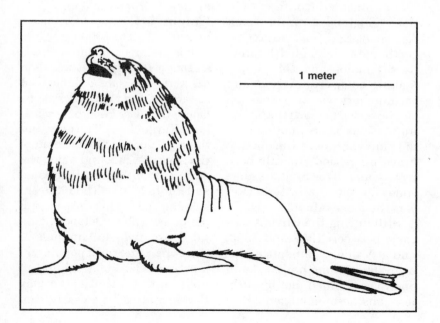

1 meter

Until the XVIII century, the navigators of the austral seas used their meat for food and their lard for the oil lamps. From then on, the demand for leather and oil in the northern hemisphere, attracted hundreds of ships to these latitudes, that year after year decimated and almost exterminated the huge Patagonian sea mammal colonies. Whales, elephant seals, one and two haired sea lions gradually disappeared from the austral seas. Alcides d'Orbigny, one of the great naturalists of the last century plainly illustrates us on the subject: "There was a rivalry among the different nations (England, France, North America). Each one wanted to get the most; they killed the pregnant females and the young, making no discrimination, and the butchery was enormous...."

They tried to reach the breeding stations before another ship did, and precisely during the breeding period, to kill both mother and offspring at the same time, for the the latter's skin was the most valuable.

Still during the current century, between 1917 and 1953, and at Valdés Peninsula alone, over 260,000 one haired sea lions were skinned, not by ruthless businessmen from other lands, but under the grant and endorsement of the national government.

From 1960 on, the hunting and selling was banned throughout the country. Luckily for them, (they had to get lucky sometime) today the animals are more profitable alive as a tourist attraction, than dead.

### SOUTHERN ELEPHANT SEAL
*Mirounga leonina*

**Order**: Pinnipedia
**Family**: Phocidae
**Size**: Males: from 4 to 5 m. - Females : from 2 to 3 m.
**Weight**: Males: up to 4 tons. - Females: 800 to 1000 kg

It is the largest of the pinnipeds and one of the largest mammals in the world. It is spread throughout Antarctica and Subantarctic islands: Orcadas, Shouthern Shetland, Kerguelen... The only continental reproductive stations of the species are found along the east coast of Valdés Peninsula and Punta Ninfas. The 1990 census, showed during the period of major assembly (October), a total figure of 43,400 animals in this zone, (the world population is estimated in 600,000), and an uplifting fact is, that it is a colony that increases 3.5% yearly, contrarily to the rest of the ones under study, that seem to have stabilized after the big killings they were submitted to. There is a small colony located near Puerto Deseado.

We have been able to see them off the coast of Rio de Janeiro, which gives us an idea of their enormous winter displacements (one animal that had been marked on the South Georgias, was found 14 months later in South Africa, 4,800 km away)

Its common name, is due to a kind of inflatable trunk that the adult males develop and that works as a resonance box to produce spectacular sounds they use to impress and drive away their possible competitors during the period they form their harems. What also calls the attention about the males are the numerous scars on their necks, that are the result of their struggle for the females. Sometimes the latter also have these marks on their back, but this time due to the the passion of copulation encounters..

Contrarily to the agility and dexterity they have in the wa-

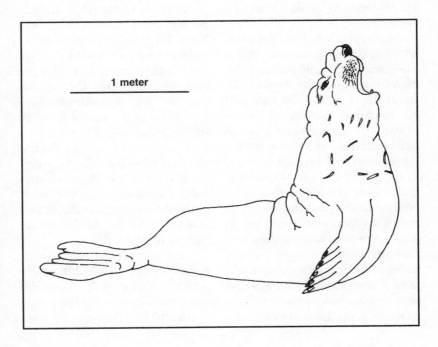

1 meter

ter, they are slow and heavy on land, because as we have already explained, they do not use their hind limbs for locomotion, and only move on the front ones, crawling with the rest of their body.

They feed especially on cephalopods (octopuses, cuttlefish, squids...) and less, on fish. They are great divers, and can reach depths of 1,500 m seeking their prey.

Their main predator is the orca, especially of the newly born and young. In Antarctic waters, they are also victims of the voracious leopard seals (Hidruga leptonyx)

In September, the first ones start arriving at the coasts for their annual reproduction cycle. Some days later the females do, and from then on each male will try to gather the largest harem it can. To the harassing of the other males, that constantly approach them to steal the loot, they respond with permanent patrolling around the seraglio and with defying snores, that scare away the competition. If this were not enough, they will fight the most aggressive rivals, fiercely biting the other male and if they should lose against another harem owner, the latter will keep the females of the loser, accumulating and serving up to 100 females per season. As it is logical, all this is carried out with great physical wearing, especially if we take into account that the constant vigilance of its treasure does not allow the male to get into the water to feed itself: therefore only few of them are able to repeat this more than two consecutive seasons. When the mating is over, towards November, the exhausted pashas will at last be able to return to the sea, where they will remain till the next mating season.

After an 11 month gestation period, the first offspring's are born. They are approximately 1 m long and weigh 40 kg., they double their weight in 11 days and 30 days later they reach 350 kg. The extraordinary content of fat of the maternal milk (80%), allows them to grow on a daily average of 10 kg during the first month of life. Also during this time, they finish changing the black nap they were born with into their adult skin, which is dark gray on the back and lighter on the belly.

The females reach their sexual maturity at 2/3 years, and the males at 6. Their life span oscillates around 20 years.

Just like all the rest of the sea

mammals, their hunting and commercialization is totally banned in Argentina.

## SOUTHERN RIGHT WHALE
### *Balaena australis*

**Order**: Cetacean (Under-order: Mysticetes)
**Family**: Balaenidae
**Size**: Males: 15 m.
Females: 16.5 m
**Weight**: Males: 40 TN.
Females: 75 TN.

The whale that swims our coasts during the summer and reproduces itself at Valdés Peninsula is one of the three under species that belong to the current classification of the black right whale. The other two correspond to the right whale of the north (B. glacialis) and of Japan (B. japonica). Together with the whale of Greenland (B. mysticetus) and the pygmy (Caperea marginata) they form the group of the right whales. Its name is due to the ancient whalers, who found in these animals all the advantages for their hunting: slow swimmers (about 3 km/h when feeding and 7/8 during migration), of a passive and trusting character, its body floats after dead, -a very appreciated advantage for their task in open sea-. The enormous amount of fat under the skin together with the other factors mentioned above, provoked the killing that has taken this species to the border of extinction, especially in the northern hemisphere.

The southern right whale is distributed throughout all the South Atlantic (it has been seen off the Brazilian coasts) though its main feeding zones are near Antarctica. To reproduce themselves, they seek calm and temperate waters, and Patagonia has the privilege of having at Valdés Peninsula an incomparable observatory to study, protect and admire these animals.

At the beginning of May, the first specimens start arriving at the Nuevo and San Jorge Gulfs, reaching the maximum number in September/October, and the last ones disappear towards the end of December.

During this period, where birth, mating and breeding of the newly born by the mother, successively take place, the whales survive thanks the nutritional reserve of their fat, for these waters lack their main food: krill, sea plankton...

The offspring is born tail first, to avoid drowning during the delivery and is immediately taken to surface by the mother. Generally, there is always another whale close by (the

1 meter

aunt, for the specialists) which helps during the delivery or simply drives away possible predators with its only presence. From then on and during a year, mother and young form an inseparable duo, as the whalers of the old days knew, so they would first harpoon the young, and afterwards await for the mother to docilely approach death in her desperate attempt to save her offspring.

When the offsprings are born, they weigh 5 TN., a weight that they double in a week, and are 5/6 m long. The young's' skin is quite light color, and goes turning black as time goes by. They reach sexual maturity at 8/9 years and their expected life span is about 40/50 years. They have an offspring every three years, which may explain the slow recovery of the species though they have been internationally protected since 1937. At Valdés Peninsula, more than 1200 animals have been identified, though only 15% returns every year (the mothers with their young and some males). The whale population (always speaking about Valdés Peninsula) seems to increase at a 7.5% annual average.

The right whale is easily identifiable by the callousness of its head and lips. Said callousness becomes populated by crustaceans and parasites thus adopting a different shape on each animal, which allows to individualize each one quite precisely. Another characteristic that, even though it is not unique to the right whales, it is more frequent than in the other cetaceans, is the spectacular leaps, where they sometimes take more than 80% of their body out of the water. There are several attempts to explain this fact, but the most accepted one attributes it to a communication code with the other individuals, a categorical way to manifest their presence in the zone. It could also be due to a way of trying to get rid of the bothersome parasites or maybe it is simply a game among the younger ones.

Regarding the subject on communication, a great variety of sounds made by the whales have been recorded. Scientists have classified them into two main purposes: communication and echolocation, to avoid obstacles and seek food.

Their dives normally last 4 to 5 minutes though they can be up to 40 in case of danger, and they generally don't reach over 150 m of depth.

## Whales and Whalers: The history of a killing

The Basques were the inventors of modern whaling. From the IX to XVI century, they had the exclusive monopoly of this commercial activity. At first, they had look outs on the coast and at the cry of "Balia, Balia", they would launch their row boats to sea. Later on, on larger vessels, they sailed all the North Atlantic, and over a century before Columbus (1372), they had already laid foot on American lands on the current Canadian peninsula of Labrador, where archaeologists have dis-

covered camps with ovens for oil manufacturing, whale squeletors, remains of barrels... Towards the XVII century, the right whale had almost been exterminated. Following the example and steps of the Basques, and many times even guided by them, the Dutch, British, Norwegians and the Danes went further north into the frozen Arctic seas. Once the "Basque Whale" had been exterminated, another species just as tame, easy and profitable, began to be the target of the European harpoons: the right whale of Greenland. abundant from parallel 60 N on, which is precisely the natural limit of the latter whale.. To avoid the "oil war", the seas were divided among the contenders (the abundance of cetaceans was enough to keep everybody happy) and each country set up its settlements on the coast from where hundreds of vessels departed every year with their holds full of barrels to illuminate the European nights.

At the beginning of the XIX century, new hunting fleets appeared: Russian, Japanese and especially North American, who would become the kings of oil and whales during that century. The naval construction, had rapidly evolved and it was then possible to rig 500 ton ships, with 6 or 7 whale boats and a crew over 40 members. Captain Acab was ready to pursue Moby Dick throughout all the corners of the seven seas and in the South Atlantic another species not yet exploited was discovered, the southern right whale. It was just as profitable as the northern ones, which continued to decrease in number. Between 1804 and 1817, two hundred thousand animals perished to the harpoons. As years before in Greenland and Terra Nova, the whalers set up their ovens and warehouses on the Antarctic continent and Subantarctic islands. Steam sailing and the invention of the harpoon cannon, would be two steps ahead in the massacre: with quick vessels and infallible explosive harpoons, new prey which had once been impossible to catch, would now shed the seas of blood. Sperm whales, rorquals and the great Blue Whale, giant of giants, all would become acquainted with the delights of the technological revolution.

The XX century will put a final corollary to the massacre: 1962 is the record year of its history: over 66,000 dead animals.

In 1946, the delegates of 19 countries (Argentina among them) create the International Whale Commission with the purpose of protecting the endangered species, create reserve zones and "scientifically" limit the captures. Full of contradictions and internal pressures from the whaling countries, (Rusia., Japan and principally Norway), extinction was so evident, that in the end, in 1982 total prohibition to hunt is voted from 1986 on.

In our days, several countries (Japan, Iceland, Norway..) are trying to abandon the Commission to be able to start hunting the supposedly not endangered species. The calvary for these giants of the sea has not yet ended.

---

(1) Though the subject and the environs of the current chapter excede the local scope of this book, that is the Argentino Lake area, I didn't want to lose the chance of writing about such a fascinating matter as the Patagonian marine fauna, which I am sure all our visitors have had or will have some contact with during their journey through these Austral lands.

I have followed the same outline for this chapter than the one chosen for the flora and fauna in the rest of the book. Since this is not addressed to specialists, but to tourists who visit Patagonia, I have not developed an exhaustive treatment on the subject.

For further information, see the bibliographical chapter at the end of these pages.

# PATAGONIAN ESTANCIAS

*A disappearing world*

A little more than a hundred years ago, Patagonia was still a *"terrae incognita"*. The absence of precious minerals was the best salvation for this zone, against eager Spanish colonizers. The small number of Indians, did not justify the troublesome expeditions to these far and inhospitable region to get cheap (or free) man power either.

Its poor soil and hard climate, left this area out of the world's economic circuit until the end of the XIX century.

During this century, a social and economic phenomenon affects the world: The Industrial Revolution. Machines of all kinds are invented and these machines have to be supplied of raw material. England is the first country to react to this fact, the British looms need an enormous amount of wool, that Europe alone cannot produce.

In 1833, the British take over the Falkland Islands, to set up a supporting port for their routes to the Pacific. (The Panama Canal would not be inaugurated till 1917, and until then, all the routes from Europe toward the Pacific ports, had to pass through the Magellan Strait or Cape Horn). Besides being a strategical support for the Empire, the always witty British, discover that those two small desolated islands in the middle of the Atlantic, were ideal for sheep raising.

The first flocks to begin sheep raising in Patagonia, will come from these islands: the first one in 1877, to some islands in the

Magellan Strait near Punta Arenas. Islands were chosen, to protect the flocks from the Tehuelches. These Indians were used to roaming freely over the steppe, and they had no sense whatsoever to what property meant, so they found in those new "white guanacos", an easy catch, much easier and tender than the fast camelids.

In 1884, when the first limit treaties with Chile, gave more secutiy to the zone, the first animals were brought to today's Santa Cruz Province. At the beginning, they only settled on the coast, later gradually, toward the inner lands. These newcomers, recieved enormous land grants from the Provincial Government, some of them up to 200,000 hectares (2,000 km2), thus beginning the latifundium tradition in Patagonia, still present in our days.

The first immigrants' origen is quite diverse: English from the Falklands, Yugoslavian or German from Punta Arenas, that at the time,was already the great ecomomic and populational center of the zone. The Argentine or Scotish foremen and administrators, brought by the great Wool Companies, ended up, in some cases, becoming the owners of the lands, when these companies abandoned the region.

All the facilities for wool producing start to be built –always near one of the scarce water courses of the zone, or by a spring– : fences, barns and houses start to rise in the desert. Rows of poplar trees and willows are planted and houses are built at their shelter. Sheep adapt at an amazing speed and the best of all is, that the world price for wool, keeps on rising.

If Darwin would pass through the area again, he could not still write his famous statement that anathematized Patagonia for a long time: "Sterility extends over the country as a real curse".

In few years, a few families concentrate the ownership of almost all of today's Santa Cruz and Tierra del Fuego Provinces in Argentina, and Magallanes in Chile, apart from the Banks, Insurance Companies, Maritime Transportation, etc. The Brauns, the Menendez, the Nogueiras... became the real czars of Patagonia and their palaces, that today can be visited in Punta Arenas, would compete with the European ones in luxury.

Only one example, can give us an idea of the power and wealth of those families:

Mauricio Braun and his sister Sara, were co-owners of the Sociedad Exportadora de Tierra del Fuego. They owned, in 1920, 1400000 hectares with 1250000 heads that produced 5000000 kilos of wool, 700000 kilos of leather and 2500000 kilos of meat annually!

The first world war, sees the apogee of wool prices (the "white gold", as it was called") that together with cotton and linen were, at the time, the only textile fibers. The technology in sheep raising was brought from England, specially from Scotland, whose administrators and foremen were great experts in handling the flocks.

The great wool companies also arrived at the Argentino Lake zone, though due to the distance to embarking centers, and hence the higher costs for transportation and supply, these lands were not as coveted as the one on the Atlantic coast, Tierra del Fuego or the Magellan Strait.

At the same time these great wool empires developed, many pioneers, adventurers and wanderers came from all over Europe to try luck in these virgin lands, but if the lands they settled on, should be interesting to the companies, they were promptly kicked out (The big fish kept eating the small one though the sea was far away). There was nothing left to do, but to gather your belongings and go West, as Percival Masters – an admirable Englishman, founder of Estancia Cristina at the Northern Arm of the Argentino Lake– said "Where no one could chase you out". This also happened to the Dane Andreas Madsen, the legendary first settler of the Chalten area, place where he settled at the beginning of the century, after being displaced several times, "willing to fight with his back against the wall". Fortunately, the wall was sturdy enough. Maybe these two men we have mentioned, are the best examples, because of their tenacity and courage, of the most praiseful virtues of the real pioneers of our zone, at the beginning of the century. The latter, has left us a most valuable book, "La Patagonia Vieja", that we highly recommend to those that want to know more about the fabulous epopee of the colonization of the Austral Cordillera.

Toward 1920, all the estancias had already settled in the zone and the way and kind of production has not changed much since then. The same animals are bred, the shearing is done with the same machinery and the wool is still exported in rough state although in recent years wool-washing industries are been established in the country.

Precisely, at that time, after the golden years, the price of the wool begins to go down. The opening of the Panama Canal, is also a big blow for the strategic importance of the zone. This will be the first economic staggering to the till then powerful wool empire and the first signs of the weakness of the model.

Second World War, means another increase in wool prices, but the progressive use of artificial textile fibers, together with the Australian, New Zealand, South African and Uruguayian competition, enlarges the offer without a consequent demand increase. These among other minor causes, will be the ones that will make the Patagonian wool progressively less profitable.

While these lines are being written, a serious danger of de-sertification threatens all Patagonia, and specially the Santa Cruz Province: the country had been overloaded by sheep at a moment, and today the mistake of an easy profit in the short run must be paid.

The constitution of the soil does not help much either to solve this problem: It has been calculated that in the Central Plateau of the province, not less than 500 years are needed to naturally recover 1 cm of thickness.

More than half the province is desertified or tends to be, and 30 % of the farming facilities have already been abandoned. More land is constantly needed per animal (in certain parts of the Central and Northern area of the province, 7 hectares –almost 14 soccer fields– are needed per head) with the consequent need for more fencing, person-nel, vehicles ... etc, which means an important increase in pro-duction costs, at an economic moment, when prices do not cease to fall. Today, the Province has 3 800 000 heads, a little over half the number of 7 000 000, that was the stock in the 50's.

The solution, unfortunately, does neither seem simple nor close.

# CALENDAR OF AN ESTANCIA

Since the estancias are usually far from the touristic circuits and it is difficult for our visitors to see the life and work carried out on them, we would like to offer a brief panorama of their activity during the year.

We will only refer to the sheep raising estancias, that are practically all the ones located in the steppe area. In the precordillera zone, due to more rainfall and better grass, the last years sheep production has been gradually changed into cattle production, usually Hereford breed, that has adapted very well to the zone. The explanation to this is, that besides its easy handling and higher profitability, cattle defend themselves better from the puma attacks, that specially roam in the mountain zone.

## SPRING

Toward September/October, the weather begins to improve in the zone. The flocks, that have been in the so called winter fields[1] during the whole winter, begin to enjoy tender grass. The sheep workers[2], go over the fields where snow gradually begins to disappear.

Parturition, starts toward October. For this to occur, it is very important to mate the animals exactly five months before, which is the gestation period, and later, to separate the males from the females during the rest of the year, in different fields, to avoid births at any other time . In more temperate zones, an animal can have three parturitions in two year (sheep can become pregnant again after the weaning, that occurs two months after the birth) but in our zone, taking into account that the production is done on open fields, this is not possible due to weather conditions.

Each mother has a lamb, (in specially chosen flocks and with good feeding, two are possible) that immediately walks next to its mother. This is the most delicate period for the animals; for the parturition, as all its life, occurs outdoors, and adverse weather conditions, like late snowfalls, or hard frosts, etc, can produce a high post-birth mortality among both mothers and lambs; specially if the winter has been very tough, and they are still weak due to a poor feeding, that is always hard to find under the snow.

This is the moment the predators have waited for, from the puma (let's recall that their cubs are also born in Spring and the mother teaches them to hunt at this time) to the fox and prey birds, they are all ready to decimate the flocks.

Once the lambs are stronger, they begin to get prepared to be driven near the main building of the estancia, where the most important jobs of the year, will be carried out; in this zone they are developed at the end of Spring and beginning of the Summer.

## SUMMER

Due to the great extensions of the estancias,[3] and therefore the great distances the flocks must travel, which tire and weaken them, they have to be moved the least possible: the first time for the summer tasks and once these are over, to the summer fields.

Unfortunately, the lack of personnel, one of the principal problems in the present estancias, does not allow all the tasks to be done at the same time. It is more and more frequent to round up the animals

first to mark them, castrate them, cut their tails, administer antiparasitic vaccines, etc, releasing them later to the field, and then having to bring them back again to the estancia for the shearing.

To carry out these round ups the sheep worker needs two indispensable tools; the horse and the dog; without them it would be impossible to move the animals.

### The Horse

The **Caballo Criollo** (creole horse), is a real Patagonian All-terrain vehicle. Though it is not as attractive as his brothers of the humid pampa, due to its strength, character and adaptability to the ground, it is an unreplaceable partner for the sheep worker. Even though today's trucks have made yesterday's great round ups disappear, when it comes to the rough ground of the zone, nothing can beat a horse.

Every estancia has a good group of them ("tropilla") that grazes freely not getting to far away from the same place ("querencia"). Only one horse is kept near the houses, ("corralero") that is saddled when the rest must be fetched.

### The sheep dog

As we have already said, dogs are the other fundamental tool for working with sheep, specially related to their driving from one place to another. It would be impossible to keep hundreds or thousands of animals together without them. Each worker has several dogs, the younger ones learn next to the older ones.

Its worth seeing these dogs at work: they are always behind their master's horse, except if he should indicate the contrary, by whistling. Their art consists in moving all the flock, keeping it always within a compact circle, and to do so, the dogs constantly run around the circle, returning any stray animal to the flock.

These animals belong to the **border-collie** breed, but today they have greatly mixed with other ones.

A good sheep dog and horse, are the most precious treasure for a **ovejero** (sheep worker).

### *The sheep shearing*

The sheepshearing is the principal moment on an estancia: All the animals are concentrated in the surroundings, the "puesteros" [4] have come from the posts to help, the shearing troop previously hired is expected. The shearers are not permanent personnel on the estancias: the shearing troops are already formed, and are integrated by shearers, wool separators, helpers, etc. that travel all over the Patagonia, beginning by the northern provinces and ending up, well in the midst of summer, in Tierra del Fuego.

They are true masters in this difficult and exhausting task (some can shear an animal in a minute and a half), their dexterity is appreciated by the estancia owners: the fleece of the sheep should be sheared in one piece, not harming the animal.

Then, the whole fleece is spread on a table where the wool is separated in two: on one side the legs and the belly, which is the dirtiest and full of powder; and on the other the flanks and loin, which is the best quality.

Then, it is taken to the bundle press. 200 to 400 kg bundles are made, ready to be loaded on the trucks that will carry them to the ports, from where they are exported, generally, with no further processing.

The mean weight of the fleece is 4 kg. in the zone (In better areas, like Magallanes in Chile or the northern part of Tierra del Fuego, they can reach 4,5 to

5 kg). The price paid at present (1999) is about $ 1 per kg.

### Pre-parturition shearing

These last few years, it has become usual in the region, to shear the animal before the parturition period, around October 15 in our zone. At this time the weather conditions improve, and late snowfalls are not very probable, because if this should happen, the animals would be left unprotected after the shearing, which could cause many losses.

The pre-parturition shearing requires an indispensable condition: **celerity**. Due to the advanced phase of gestation (10 to 15 days before birth), the mother cannot be more than 4 hours fasting, without running a serious risk for the life of the fetus. If we consider, that to shear: first we have to put the animals in the several corrals near the shearing barn, then distribute them among the shearers, shear them and them drive them back to the field, it is

easy to understand the indispensable coordination that is needed to carry out this task with the great number of animals involved and without wasting time.

Besides, the animals have to be treated with **great care**, during, before and after the shearing, for example, it is not possible to work with dogs, to avoid stress and violent movements of the flock.

Taking into account that the shearers are not permanent personnel, it is also necessary their **absolute punctuality** the day the shearing is to begin, because the animals are already separated near the estancia, where feeding is not very abundant.

There are great advantages to the pre-parturition shearing over the traditional one, both regarding the quality of the wool and the lambs. The difficult winter conditions (climate, scarce food ..) create a general stress situation in the animals that shows in the strangulating of

Post parturation Shearing

Pre parturation Shearing

CUTTING

**WOOL FIBERS**

the wool fibers. The pre-parturition shearing, since it is done after winter, allows to cut the fiber close to the strangulation point, thus giving the wool more consistency (hence a higher price) because it avoids having the weakest point in the middle of the fiber.

Another advantage is, that when the spring winds begin in the zone, the animal's fleece will still be short, avoiding less concentration of powder and filth, which is another factor that reduces the quality and price of the wool.

After the shearing, since the animal does not have its natural protection, it will develop a very beneficial behavior for the future lamb.

On one hand, it will eat more than habitual, and therefore the fetus will develop more, specially in the last part of its gestation, gaining considerable weight. On the other hand, the mother will look for a more sheltered spot to give birth, creating better conditions for the newly born and thus a higher rate of survival in the flock.

Besides, the early shearing, makes it possible to drive the flocks to the high summer fields, that as we have already said, are the largest ones and less used due to the hard weather conditions. This way, there is more time for the winter fields to rest and recover.

### Antiparasitic bath

Some days after the shearing, another annual job is undergone, the bath, which is essential for the good health of the flock because it combats parasites, specially mange and sheep tick.

The task is done in a sort of cement channel that is filled with water, and where the antiparasitic products are dissolved in. The animals are forced to swim along the channel. A worker with a special kind of fork, sinks their heads one by one, to be sure all the body is wet. The animals come out of the channel to some cement corrals, where they dry themselves before they are set free again.

As long as more estancias administer injectable vaccines, the bathing job will gradually disappear.

### Marking

The lambs' ears are marked with the owner's characteristic mark. Since the animals are all together, the occasion is also used to mark them with different paint spots to later be able to identify their sex, age, etc, when they are in the field.

### Castration and tail cutting

Only a very small percentage of males are kept for reproduction (about 3 %). Almost all the lambs will be castrated to produce more fattening.

As we have already said, after the shearing, the wool is separated according to its cleanness. The animal's tail is cut at the same time it is castrated, to avoid that with its long tail it soils its rear part.

After all these tasks are over, the animals are ready to be driven to the high or summer fields, where they will be for 3 or 4 months before they come back near the estancias.

## AUTUMN

During the rest of the summer and the autumn, the old animals will be replaced by the young ones[5], for as we have said, each land, according to the conditions it is submitted to, can bear a certain number of animals, and to overload it with a greater number, would only mean the estancia's owner's ruin.

At this time of year, the lambs up to a year old, which are famous all over the country for their flavor, are sold. The kind of grass, together with the fact that the animals are obliged to constantly walk to be able to feed themselves, give the lamb from Santa Cruz an incomparable taste.

The typical way to prepare it, is known as " cordero al palo", and is done by sticking an iron bar through the open animal (in the old days a green branch was used, and the name "palo" comes from that fact) and sticking that bar in the earth before a great fire. The heat cooks the meat slowly, as the fat slips to the ground. The results are: a gastronomic delicatessen that we will never get tired of recommending our visitors.

February 15, is the town anniversary, in honor of the naming of the Lake by the Perito Moreno, and a celebration in Calafate. One of the most popular events of the day is the simultaneous barbecuing of 100 animals!! for the delight of the town people and tourists as well; all they have to do is to come with a knife and eat until they satiate.

### Mating

Around the middle of autumn, toward the beginning of May approximately, the service or cover of the females by the males is done. The relation is about one male every 25 females. It is important to do it on the correct dates above mentioned, for the parturitions to commence at the end of September / beginning of October, when weather conditions allow high percentages of survival.

### Eye shearing

Another task that is done toward the end of autumn, (April, May), after the sheep have come down to the winter fields, is the "eye shearing". Due to the abundant wool that has grown from the summer shearing on the animal's head, around the eyes, it is necessary to trim it to avoid that, snow, branches and thistle, accumulate thus impairing its vision, not allowing it to graze and walk.

Another eye shearing is done, toward the end of winter (August, September).

# WINTER

Winter is the calmest time of the year, regarding work on the estancia: Except for the sheep workers surveillance travels over the fields and some maintanence job, activity is minimum.

With the first snowfalls, when the tracks are easily followed by the dogs, the men go puma hunting. Together with the puma, the great snowfall is the other cause for the high winter mortality in the flocks. The animals, frozen stiff, because of the cold, and not able to find food, gather tightly one against each other in great groups, until they end up suffocating one's another; or due to their weakness they lay down on the snow ground, and end up definitely stuck to it because of the frost, dying from cold and inanition. To avoid this, the horse troop goes all over the fields, digging and opening trails in the snow for the sheep to go through and be able to eat.

Another winter task, is to make holes on the frozen streams and water holes, to allow the animals to drink water.

The workers may also profit from this compulsory idle season preparing their fox traps; for some of them the selling of the fox skins can mean an extra salary.

And speaking of predators, another plague that has decimated the flocks these last years around Calafate, are domestic dogs, that forming packs, go sheep hunting during the night to the neighboring estancias, coming home in the morning, where during the daytime they lead normal lives at their master's home.

Winter mortality on an estancia varies greatly, due to the reasons mentioned above. A 10/15 percent is normal, but during very hard winters it can reach up to 30/40 percent.

(1) In this zone, due to the hard winters and the poor grass, the estancias usually have two kinds of fields: the summer fields, that are usually located in the high valleys and plateaus, and the winter ones, near Argentino Lake and the Santa Cruz River. The first are usually larger (three to four times than the winter ones) which is a problem for the economic exploitation of the estancia, because due to the hard weather conditions, the flocks have to spend most of the year in the smaller fields.

(2) There are two kinds of estancia worker: the one that is in charge of maintenance, cleaning, cooking, etc and that carries out his work on foot; and the "ovejero" (Sheep worker) that goes over the fields on horseback, checking the fences and watching over the animals. If he should find a dead animal, that was attacked by a puma or another animal, or which had an accident (in winter, it is frequent that because of ice or snow animals slip and fall into canyons or down cliffs where they are trapped), he must remove its hide and leave it drying on the nearest fence. That is why, sometimes you can see hides hanging from the fences along the road.
When he goes out into the country, he also checks the traps he has set up, and he may come back with a fox skin that he will trade or sell to a merchant that periodically visits the estancias called " mercachifle", and who is a real ambulant salesman of the very few luxuries a "gaucho" has: cheap clothes, boots, soap and a comb, tobacco, yerba mate, gin...

(3) 3 to 4 hectares are needed per animal (In the province of Buenos Aires, 85 heads can be raised on the same surface !) and the estancias in the zone can have from 4000 to 30000 animals. Taking into account that 1 km2 is equal to 100 hectares, it is easy to calculate the immensities needed for any exploitation.

(4) As we have already said, the estancias have great extensions of territory that can not be controlled from the main building. Therefore, small houses or posts ("puestos") are built, scattered over all the surface of the estancia, where a solitary "puestero" lives in the company of his horse and dogs. He watches over his section, going to the estancia once in awhile to fetch his provisions or "vicios" (vices): sugar, yerba, salt...

(5) In this zone, due to the hard grass, the sheep's teeth wears in 4 or 5 years, which is the animals useful life. After this time, the animal must be necessarily replaced, if not it would die of inanition.

Cerro Torre

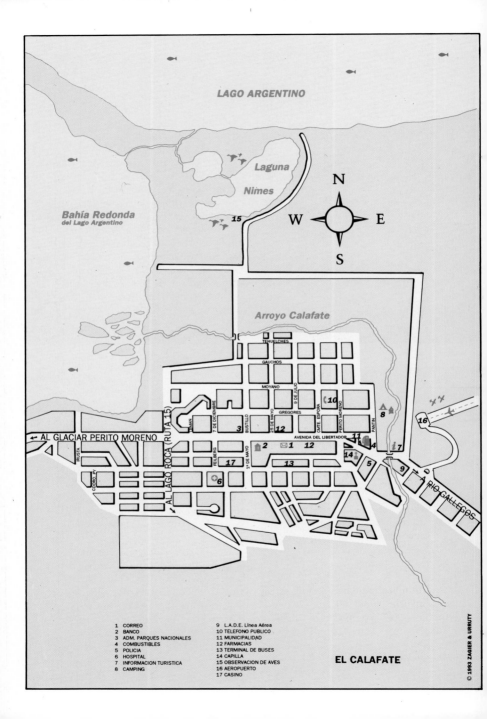

LAGO ARGENTINO

Laguna
Nimes

Bahía Redonda
del Lago Argentino

15

N
W        E
S

Arroyo Calafate

TEHUELCHES
GAUCHOS
MOYANO
9 DE JULIO
← AL GLACIAR PERITO MORENO
GREGORES            10
BUSTILLO
3          12
AVENIDA DEL LIBERTADOR
2          1    12        11  4
17          13        14   5   7
6                           9

AL LAGO ROCA (RUTA 15)
7 DE DICIEMBRE
9 DE MAYO
COMTE. ESPORA
PERITO MORENO
PANTIN
8
16
AL RIO GALLEGOS

1   CORREO
2   BANCO
3   ADM. PARQUES NACIONALES
4   COMBUSTIBLES
5   POLICIA
6   HOSPITAL
7   INFORMACION TURISTICA
8   CAMPING
9   L.A.D.E. Línea Aérea
10  TELEFONO PUBLICO
11  MUNICIPALIDAD
12  FARMACIAS
13  TERMINAL DE BUSES
14  CAPILLA
15  OBSERVACION DE AVES
16  AEROPUERTO
17  CASINO

EL CALAFATE

© 1993 ZAGIER & URRUTY

# THE MATE

Just like we have talked about the horse and the dog as irreplaceable tools for the working men on the estancias, we would also like refer to another loyal and indispensable friend during leisure i.e. the mate.

It is of customary use in Argentina and the bordering countries, as well as in this area, and specially on the estancias. The day begins and ends with the mate, it is a treat for the guests, a company while chatting around the fire. Its friendly bitterness will just as well do on finishing a good barbecue or to mitigate the endless winter nights on the solitary posts.

## History

The mate has been drunk since immemorial times by the Guarani indians, at the beginning as a simple potion they filtered through their teeth, and later on by using a dry squash as a recipient and a stem of a rush to sip it up.

Mate leaves have been found in the Incan graves, which confirms its use among this Pre Hispanic culture.

At first, the Jesuit missionaries tried to forbid it in the Argentine-Paraguayan converted indian settlements, (it seems that the indian doctors, would inhale the smoke of the dry leaves, and pretend to communicate with the spirits and foretell the future), but soon they discovered in its tonic properties a sane substitute for alcohol, that was already causing ravage among the indian population of that time. The Jesuits were also the ones who promoted and almost monopolized its cultivation, and even introduced great innovations in its elaboration. In their attempt to introduce it into the Old Continent, they took it to Spain where it was called "The Jesuit Tea". But after the expulsion of the Order by Charles III, its consumption was easily displaced by the tea that the British brought from the Asian colonies.

During the Colony, its use was a lot more spread out than it is nowadays, reaching up to northern Chile, Peru, Bolivia and Ecuador. But the price raise to the end of the XVIII century, gradually reduced its consumption to the current limits.

### The Plant

The *mate* is a shrub (*llex paraguaiensis, llex mate...*) of the family of the Aquifoliaceous. also known as lilaceous. It can reach 6 meters when cultivated and pruned, and up to 10 m in its natural state, that is why it can be considered a tree.

Besides the several mineral salts, citric and ascorbic acids in its chemical composition, the leaves contain about 1% of caffeine, which gives the herb its tonic and stimulating character and also explains why the Guaranies drank it as an antidote against fatigue and hunger.

There are several steps to follow from its gathering to its arrival at the market. The herb is dried with electric dryers or with fire, in this last case it is very important to avoid smoke, which would ruin the flavor. Then it is crushed and sifted in different sizes, according to the taste of each country.

### Geography

Today, mate is drunk in all Argentina, Uruguay, Paraguay, southern Brazil and Chile. Though the herb comes from very similar plants, each region adds its own variations: sweetened with sugar or honey, aromatized with herbs, cold in Paraguay (variety known as terere)... etc.

In our part of the country it is usually drunk bitter, that is only the herb without any additional element.

### Drinking Mate

Though the mate herb is simply an infusion, its peculiarity comes from the way it is drunk. In the first place, it requires a certain atmosphere of friendship and conviviality among the people who drink it and of a certain relaxed "time". It is not drunk with anybody nor in passing or in a hurry like a coffee; that is why, though it is very popular, it is restricted to the home environment and it is impossible to find it in any public place.

The utensils you use to drink it are: a mate (generally a hollowed dry squash). a "*bombilla*" or metal sucking straw, that has some holes in its bottom end to filter the herb, a kettle or tea pot to pour the water from. It is important to never let the water boil, because this would spoil the herb.

You fill half the mate with the herb, you pour in the hot water to swell the herb and afterwards you introduce the "*bombilla*".

The same person always "*ceba*" the mate (i.e. pours the water into the mate), usually the host, who passes it on to each of the members of the group, that after sucking up the content, returns it to the "*cebador*", who refills it again and hands it to the next person.

After some "*cebadas*", which depend on the quantity and quality of the herb, the latter starts to lose its flavor and therefore the drinking is over.

# TWO MOUNTAINS, TWO LEGENDS, TWO CONQUESTS.

## Lionnel Terray, Guido Magnone and the Conquest of Fitz Roy

*"When alone in the calmness and warmth of my home, I let my spirit wander astray among the memory of so many images and adventures, the peaks of Patagonia appear before me so unreal, so fabulously shaped, that I believe that these images have come out of some mad dream"*

*Lionnel Terray*

The Fitz Roy or Chalten, was quoted in all the chronicles and narration's of the explorers of Austral Patagonia, but it was known in the climbing milieu thanks to Father Alberto María de Agostini, who had an out-standing performance in the area for his remarkable explorations (we owe most of the toponymy of Italian origin to him). The tall peaks of the Alps had already been defeated by that time, so the priest's pictures would awake the climbing European elites' desires for new challenges elsewhere, i.e. to conquer that " Unbeaten King of Patagonia".

In 1937, the first attack towards the summit was launched by an Italian expedition but it did not even reach the base of the wall. There would be other attempts later on, but nobody was able to find the weak side of the inaccessible granite bastion.

In 1950, a French expedition reached the top of the Annapuma, in the Himalayan

Cordillera. It is the first "eight thousand " tread made by mankind and one of the great successes in the history of mountain climbing. It will be Lionnel Terray, " the Locomotive of the Alps " and several of the members of that expedition who, in December 1951, weigh anchor from Paris and sail to Buenos Aires, with two and a half tons of equipment and the most daring dream that a mountain climber could have at that time: the conquest of the Fitz Roy.

They were welcomed with great honors by the then President Perón (who also had a mountaineer background in the Andes and the Alps). The Argentine government puts transport and communication means at the group's disposal, to facilitate the operative.

Before starting the ascension, a tragedy occurs: Jacques Poincenot, one of the great climbers of his time, drowns while trying to wade across the Fitz Roy River, some few meters away from the present concrete bridge near the town of Chalten. One of the most beautiful neighboring peaks to Fitz Roy, would later be named after him. However, there is another version of his death among the inhabitants of the zone: Poincenot was killed by a jealous estancia owner, whose wife had been seduced by the handsome Frenchman.

On January 5, 1952, after almost ten days of transporting, fording and conveying, they start setting up their base camp on the left coast of the Blanco River, protected by the forests, from the winds that scourged the region, a minor prelude to what awaited them further on. Some rustic cabins are built out of fallen trees; the few existing clearings are cleaned up to set up the tents, logs are arranged to be used as tables and chairs..., everything is arranged trying to make this inhospitable place as habitable as possible for it would be used for a month, as a home and a support base for the attack to the summit.

The expedition is deployed into several fronts: while some start carrying load to the upper camps, the geographer and physicist Louis Lliboutry makes cartography of the zone (we owe him the names of the peaks that escort the colossus and that are dedicated to the pioneers of the French aviation: Saint-Exupéry, Mermoz, Guillaumet...)

A scout group starts exploring the itinerary they should follow between the base camp and the base of the wall. They tried to open a path between the crevices and seracs, marking the trail that later would be permanently used upward and downward, to set up the height camps with all the necessary elements: provisions, ropes, climbing gear, fuel... This was a slow and tiresome technique, but the only one at the time that could assure the success of such an objective, with the available material.

The so called height camps, were simple caverns dug in the snow and ice, where one or two tents were set up, and a small space to cook was arranged. Inside the caverns, the men could tolerate the weather conditions that otherwise would make surviving impossible.

Fifteen days after the expedition had begun, and after superhuman efforts against a wind none of them had ever known throughout their long mountaineering experience, they had a discouraging balance: on the first real climbing day, they were only able to achieve twenty of the 700 meters to the top. The technical difficulties surpassed what they had anticipated and moreover the terrible wind scourged the mountain, with deafening and dantesque gusts.

They were growing short on provisions and fuel.. after a great snowfall, that even concealed one of the caverns they used as a height camp, all the expeditionaries gathered again at the base camp. Neither the barbecues or gin that the estancia owners would generously contribute with were enough to mitigate the feeling of defeat that soared over the expedition. Madsen's prophesy, was being fulfilled: according to it, the Fitz Roy was a mountain that God had placed on Earth to destroy man's pride and mark the ultimate limit to his possibilities.

On January 28, a hopeful wind from the southeast, a bearer of good weather as the local people would say, encourages the camp again.

Everything starts all over again with renewed impetus: the mountain sees that procession of stubborn visionaries parade upwards once more. They supply the camps of provisions again and three days later, Terray and Magnone, the attack group, are on the wall again. They slowly drive wood pegs and stoppers in the cracks and thus rig 120 meters of vertical wall. They slide down the fixed ropes, that will allow them to get back there quickly the next day, and sleep again in their ice cavern at the base of the wall.

The next day, there is still good weather, and the climbers feel that the moment has come. It is now or never. This is not a mountain that gives second chances. They start out with the minimum weight, that never is such. They would have to sleep on the wall that night, and in the morning, if all goes well, launch the final attack, they risk all, the most dangerous bet they have made in their lives. The climb is exhausting but slowly they go up along the cracks and slabs. They sleep on a tiny platform, tied to the wall with ropes and pegs. The night is not very cold and the wind is calm.

After only a drink of water and some lumps of sugar, the day they had waited for so long begins. The distant tops are covered by clouds and the worst omen blows over the abysses: the fearful west wind. The difficulties do not diminish, the wind blows harder and harder. For the first time in his life, Lionnel feels defeated: the great Terray, the living legend of mountain climbing of his time, admired in Nepal by the very sherpas because of his physical resistance, and undoubtedly one of the great ones of all times, decides to withdraw.

His partner Guido Magnone, stricken by madness (for you cannot call his idea of going onwards in those conditions any other way), takes the lead at that moment, and is the one to keep the flame of conquest burning. No risk is too great to take, the key is celerity and his expertise on the rock is fundamental.

At the total limit of his resistance, with no pegs to secure themselves, without having drunk or eaten anything in the last 48 hours, at 5 p.m. February 2, 1952, both men embrace each other on the top.

The material reward to so much effort? A tiny stone as a souvenir that each one puts in his pocket before starting down. The spiritual one is something I suggest each reader should decide for him or herself.

## Cesare Maestri and the Torre Peak: A mith of stone

The traveler that approaches the peaks of the Cordillera from the steppe, will undoubtedly be firstly attracted to the imposing mass of the Fitz Roy. Due to its height that surpasses the surrounding peaks and its perfect shape, resembling a proud pyramid, the mountain has an excluding magnetism, that hardly allows you to appreciate any other around it, when you see the whole formation from afar.

But once in the midst of the cordillera, another mountain stands out with a light of its own: the Torre. The first mountaineers to approach it, could not avoid qualifying it with the most frightening adjectives such as: the damned mountain, the petrified scream, the gelid hell, the impossible crest... Dr. Azema, physician of the French expedition to Fitz-Roy described before, wrote in his diary " To only think of climbing it is vane and ridiculous".

Once the Fitz Roy had been defeated, this was a new challenge for the eternal searchers of virgin peaks. Though lower than the latter, the Torre peak had much greater technical problems to solve: the damp winds from the Pacific and the sudden storms, the vertical walls that could be covered with snow in a few hours and with the same speed, after a slight heating up, collapse in enormous sheets irremediably trapping whoever should be climbing it at that moment. These were more than enough factors to justify the legendary adjectives that accompanied its name.

From the first attempts, the Torre became a kind of Italian competition: the great climbers of that nationality made it a real race to the top where polemics and rivalry were not absent.

In 1957, two Italian expeditions tried to reach the top: from the west side the expedition leaded by Bonatti and Mauri, one of the great climbing couples in the history of mountain climbing, reached a small hill they called " Saddle of Hope" which separates the Torre from the Adela Peak. One hundred meters further up, they lost their hope of succeeding, because the technical difficulties and storms obliged them to turn back. The expedition that went up the east wall had the same luck: "The Torre Peak is an impossible mountain, and for the safety of all, I forbid you to keep on trying". These were the words uttered by the leader of the group, the famous Bruno Detassi.

One of the members of this last expedition, Cesare Maestri, "The Spider of the Dolomites", felt that his fate was so bound to the mountain, that during the sad retreat, he wrote the following in his diary: "We are here with the feeling that we have left something unfinished behind . But I believe I have done everything possible to avoid this from happening. I must return and I will".

Two years later, we find Maestri before his obsession again, about to start out what would be one of the most confusing pages in the history of mountain climbing, marked with tragedy and polemics: the first ascension to the Torre.

During the first days, they carried all the material through the valley of the Fitz Roy River, to the base of the wall. Once the three camps had been set up, one at Torre Lake, the other at the foot of the Mocho and the third at 1650 meters altitude, and the projections had been rigged with fixed ropes, the expedition withdrew to the base camp at Torre Lake to await the good weather.

On January 28, 1959, they decided to attack: Cesare Maestri, Cesarino Fava and Toni Egger advanced fast along the fixed ropes and in eleven hours reached a hill on the north face that they baptized with the name of "Collado de la Conquista" (Saddle of the Conquest) in opposition to the "Collado de la Esperanza" (Saddle of Hope) that Bonatti and Mauri had reached years before on the south side. "Hope is the weapon of the weak" Mae-

stri had stated when he referred very openly to his former rivals. The first night they slept there, and the next morning Fava went down to the base camp while Egger and Maestri continued upward.

Some of the paragraph's from the latter's diary, give us the idea of the nightmare atmosphere which surrounded them "...the north wall rises vertiginously before us. Plates, grooves, cracks, are all covered with a sheet of iced snow, that seems false and provisional to us. Toni looks at me; I remain quiet. Thus our struggle begins..." "sometimes large areas covered with snow sink as the wind blows giving us the chills". After twelve hours, where every instant could have been the last, the two climbers arrived at a small snow landing on the ice, where they are able to set up a precarious bivouac, under the iced mushroom formations on the top. "The night goes by fast, the weather is fine and only the will to fight is kept in mind", writes Maestri.

Another day that brings more dangers and uncertainty, the same vertical sheets of ice pending over them like the swords of Damocles about to fall. Another night hanging from the walls, this time only two hundred meters from the top. Before sunset, the mountain formations of the Pacific start to get covered by clouds, the temperature rises, the barometer goes down.. all are unmistakable signs of the tempest from the west that is closing on over them. The next day will not only be a struggle against the mountain but against the clock as well.

I give Maestri the floor again: "Toni starts out and surpasses a very steep wall, almost vertical. He goes up driving one spike in after another. He goes over an ice salient and screams: "Cesare! ... the top!"

So many months of preparations and dreams, so much effort and risk and in the end of all, some brief seconds on the top surrounded by the tempest. What starts then, more than a descent is desperate escape downward. The wind blows harder and harder and the snow sheets weaken and collapse all around.

Another bivouac, the fifth, and the next day they get back to the Collado de la Conquista, (Saddle of the Conquest) at last protected from the wind...but not from the avalanches, that keep falling from the mountain above: almost reaching the fixed ropes, "...While I descend, writes Maestri, a deafening sound makes me look up: a huge mass of snow and ice separates from the wall. I yell: Toni, be careful" and I stick my back against the the wall. I feel a dry blow, the rope gets tense, the avalanche strikes Toni and covers him... Afterwards, everything stops: I can only hear the howling wind, while I recover the weightless rope..."

The tragedy that persecuted them since they had set foot on that damned mountain , had made its deadly blow the last moment, when the salvation of the fixed ropes was at the reach of their hands . The night is endless: alone and exhausted, at dawn he starts the descent: "Today my life will be decided on. I will not look up if a harder gust warns me that the avalanche will fall. I will not scream if everything in an instant turns tense and silent. I will not be able to feel happy if I reach the base".

If the ascension had been a nightmare, the return to his country was not a rose garden either for Maestri: some of the mountain climbing media start to doubt his narration. The pictures of the top, the only probatory document, were in Toni Egger's camera (four years later some English climbers found the body in the Torre Glacier, but no signs of the camera). Since he cannot prove his assertions he is accused of being a liar. A polemic begins.

The myth of the Torre grew day after day: The best mountain climbers of the world urged to conquest it; English and Italians would launch each ones attacks by the east and the west, that failed on account of the bad weather and the eternal extreme difficulties the granitic crag defended itself with, from all its sides.

In 1970, again Maestri, criticized, sour and hurt in his pride, would return to the Torre to settle the revenge he had so long waited for; his proposal is both challenging and crazy: to climb the Torre in winter, when the wind ceases in Patagonia and the weather, though colder, also becomes more stable.

Maestri did not curtail means on his enterprise: some of the technical innovations he conceived for that occasion are currently used in mountain climbing today; such as the boots with double outer plastic or the coats with inner aluminum lining. But the most outrageous idea of all and due to which Maestri would once again arise a wave of criticism and polemics in the mountain world, was no less than the use of a compressor to fix the spikes by pressure into the wall. Ignorant of all the scandals his boldness had provoked, Maestri and his expedition would carry a hundred and eighty kilos of machine, tools, tubes and fuel upward, besides the necessary material for an ascension of the kind. Like a Fitzcarraldo of verticality, Maestri is a delirium that only looks upward; he wrote in his diary shortly before commencing the ascension: "... and from now on the days will not be minutes or hours but only centimeters and meters".

However, again it would be the weather, this time in the form of intense snowfalls, that would stop Maestri four hundred meters from the top.

Back in Italy, that sort of heretic of climbing he had become according to many, started to prepare his return, and that same summer of 1970, we would find him there again, to end what he had started.

At last a series of days with good weather and on December 2, that sort of dream-nightmare that had hallucinated him for so many years. "Ghe son !, Ghe son!" (Here we are, here we are) he yells together with his partners. They had reached the limit of the difficulties of rock and the characteristic mushroom of ice that covers the Torre rose before them. Because he did not consider it as forming part of the mountain (it can fall any day, Maestri had sentenced), neither did he have the appropriate material for doing it, Maestri and his partners did not trespass the final meters of ice, which of course would add more fuel to the fire of the polemics that the many enemies of this famous climber permanently anathematized him with.

Having or not reached the top, a crucial page of his life had been closed and also one of the most intense and discussed chapters in the history of mountaineering: the Torre Peak had been defeated.

# BIBLIOGRAPHY

**BOOKS AND ARTICLES**

- *Trekking en Chaltén & Lago del Desierto*
  Zagier & Urruty Publications. M. Alonso

- *Los Glaciares*
  Editorial Time-Life. Ronald H. Bailey.

- *Los Períodos Glaciares*
  Ed. Widsord Chorlton.

- *Historia Marítima Argentina*
  Dpto. Estudios Históricos Navales.

- *Hielo Patagónico Sur*
  Instituto de la Patagonia. Mateo Martinic.

- *Historia de Santa Cruz*
  Ed. Alberto Raúl Segovia. Juan H. Lenzi.

- *Viajes a la Patagonia Austral*
  Editorial Solar. F.P. Moreno.

- *Vida entre los patagones*
  Editorial Solar. G.CH. Musters.

- *Anales del Instituto de la Patagonia*
  Inst. de la Patagonia. Punta Arenas.

- *Glaciar Moreno*
  Servicio Meteorológico Nacional. Raffo - Colqui - Madesjki.

- *El Ventisquero Moreno*
  Rev. La Ingeniería. C. Volpi - A. Grandi.

- *Southern Patagonia: Glacial Events*
  Between 4 m.y. and 1 m.y. Ago. Mercer - Fleck - Sander.

- *Plan Regulador de Calafate - 1969*
  Com. de Fomento. J.M. Pastor - J. Bonilla.

- *Glaciological Researches in Patagonia*
  Universidad de Hokkaido - 1990. P. Skvarca - Narusse - Aniya.

- *La Patagonia trágica*
  Zagier & Urruty Publications. J.M. Borrero.

- *Los vengadores de la Patagonia trágica*
  Hyspamérica. Osvaldo Bayer.

- *Conociendo Torres del Paine*
  Gladys Garay - Oscar Guineo.

- *La Patagonia Vieja*
  Zagier & Urruty Publications. Andreas Madsen.
- *Guía para la Identificación de Aves de Argentina y Uruguay*
  Editorial Vazquez Mazzini. T. Narosky - D. Yzurieta.
- *Aspectos Glaciológicos de la Zona del Hielo Continental Patagónico*
  Editorial Instituto Nacional del H.C.P. Mario Bertone.
- *Descripción Geológica de la Patagonia*
  E. Feruglio.
- *Pequeña Flora Ilustrada de los Parques Nacionales andino-patagónicos*
  Milán Jorge Dimitri.
- *Fauna Argentina*
  Constancio Vigil.
- *Investigación Histórica sobre los Tehuelches*
  Municipalidad de Cmte. Luis Piedrabuena -
  Santa Cruz. Marcos Scurzi.
- *Al Asalto del Fitz-Roy*
  Editorial Peuser. Louis Depasse.
- *Cuadernos Patagónicos III y IV*
  Techint.
- *Mate, símbolo de amistad*
  Zagier & Urruty Publications. C. Vairo
- *El mate, su historia y su cultura*
  Editorial Del Sol. Margarita Barreto.
- *Huellas en la arena, sombras en el mar*
  Editorial Terra Nova. Alfredo A. Lichter.
- *La vie au bout du monde*
  Editorial Flammarion. Cousteau - Paccalet.
- *La planète des baleines*
  Editorial R. Laffont. Cousteau - Paccalet.

## MAPS ZAGIER & URRUTY
- *Parque Nacional Los Glaciares*
- *Monte Fitz Roy / Cerro Torre / Lago del Desierto*

## ACKNOWLEDGMENT

I'd like to thank **Mr. Julio Cabanas, Mr. Pedro Jankielewicz, Mr. Horacio Suetaz, Mr. Sañin Simunovic** and **Mr. Claudio Roig** for their invaluable help and information about the zo. e.

# SERVICES, TOURS & TREKKING GUIDE

## Los Glaciares National Park

•

## El Calafate

•

## El Chaltén

Patagonia is a place full of dinamics and changes. Due to that, a wider spectrum is offered every year to the traveler. As frecuencies and prices of services can change as well from one year to another, we recommend our visitors to check in advance with the local Information Services of the area. The author, who resides in the area, has prepared an updated guide of useful data for 1999 (from the Editor).

Legend:
- – – – International Boundary
- —— Paved Road
- —— Unpaved Road
- ······· Route 40 (Pelque River)

## DISTANCES MEASURED IN KILOMETERS

+ Via National Route 40 (Pelque River)

* Via Cancha Carrera

(1) Distance to Torres del Paine National Park is considered to the Main Office.

| | | | | | | |
|---|---|---|---|---|---|---|
| **EL CALAFATE** | | | | | | |
| 225 | | | | | | |
| **EL CHALTEN** | 300+ | | | | | |
| 440+ | 320 | | | | | |
| **RIO TURBIO** | 490 | 290+ | | | | |
| 250 | 445+ | 570 | | | | |
| **RIO GALLEGOS** | 25 | 695 | 330* | | | |
| 275 | 265 | 475+ | 900 | | | |
| **PTO. NATALES** | 260 | 175 | 1050 | | | |
| 250 | 380* | 770 | | | | |
| **PTA. ARENAS** | 150 | 620 | | | | |
| 400 | 750 | | | | | |
| **T. DEL PAINE (1)** | 500 | | | | | |
| 900 | | | | | | |
| **USHUAIA** | | | | | | |

# TRAVEL SERVICES

# EL CALAFATE

## LAND TRANSPORTATION

### *RIO GALLEGOS - CALAFATE - RIO GALLEGOS*

| | |
|---|---|
| *Distance:* | 320 km |
| *Road:* | Paved |
| *Frequency:* | Daily, all year round. |
| *Duration:* | 4 hours |
| *Departures:* | In Río Gallegos, from the Bus Terminal or the Airport. In El Calafate, also from Bus Terminal. |
| *Price:* | u$s 25 |
| *Schedule:* | Early in the morning (from 6 to 8 AM) from Calafate to Río Gallegos and at about 2 PM from Río Gallegos to Calafate. The schedules are modified during the year, because they adjust to plane departures and arrivals at Río Gallegos Airport. |

### *CALAFATE - PERITO MORENO GLACIER - CALAFATE*

| | |
|---|---|
| *Distance:* | 80 km |
| *Road:* | Gravel |
| *Frequency:* | Daily, all year round |
| *Departures:* | 9 AM in Summer, 10 AM in Winter |
| *Price:* | u$s 25. Price includes bilingual English - Spanish guide, but not entrance fee to the National Park (u$s 5) |
| *Schedule:* | 8 hrs. approximately, round grip. |

From Calafate, it takes about 2 and a half hours to get to the Glacier, stopping several times for picture taking. The visitors have about 3 hours time to walk the pathways that take to all the viewpoints where the glacier can be admired from.

*Lunch:*     There are two restaurants: **Los Nostros**, 5 m before the pathways with excellent pamoramic views of the Glacier and U.T.V.M. (Unidad Turística Ventisquero Moreno) that counts with two facilities: a restaurant 500 m from the pathways and a snack bar at the very pathways.

## CALAFATE - CHALTEN

*Distance:*

*Road:*     225 km

*Frequency:*     33 km paved and the rest gravel

*Schedule:*     Daily from Nov. to Apr. In Oct. and May, 3 times a week, and the rest of the year 2/3 times a month.

*Duration:*     Early in the morning from Calafate (6 or 7 AM.) and around 4 PM from Chalten back to Calafate.

*Price:*     3 and a half hours.

     u$s 50 (round trip)

## CHALTEN - LAGO DEL DESIERTO

The same bus lines that operate the transfers from Calafate, organize an extension trip up to the south margin of Lago del Desierto (Desierto Lake) located 37 km from El Chaltén along a winding gravel road. The trip costs u$s 10 and the duration (round trip) is 2 hours. It is possible to sail the lake from the southern coast up to the very northern zone. Check prices and schedules in Chaltén.

## CALAFATE - PUERTO NATALES

*Distance:*     380 km

*Frequency:*     Daily

*Price:*     u$s 30 (one way)

---

## AIR TRANSPORTATION

Both Líneas Aéreas del Estado (LADE) as well as Kaikén Líneas Aéreas fly Río Gallegos - Calafate, continuing afterwards up to Tierra del Fuego or the northern part of the country. Both the flight frequencies as well as the destinations are very changeable according to the time of the year.

## TOURS AND EXCURSIONS

Undoubtedly, the most important tourist attraction of the region and a must, is the visit to the **Perito Moreno Glacier.**, a brief description can be found in the Land Transportation Chapter, in this same section. Besides the visit to the pathways and view points, we suggest the visitor two other options in the Glacier area.

### *Nautical Safari*

A short boat ride, on a comfortable craft, with plenty of indoor and outdoor space, about one hour long, along the southern front of the Glacier. Interesting panoramic views of the ice wall, from the Lake Cost u$s 20.

### *Minitrekking on the Moreno Glacier*

A unique experience and an excellent chance to know the Glacier from a different scope, i.e. a safe trekking on the very glacier.

5 km before the pathways, you embark to cross to the other side of the Rico Arm (the same embarking pier as the Nautical Safari). On the other shore, specialized mountain guides greet the visitors and lead them to the very edge of the Glacier. There after placing spikes on their footwear, the group goes onto the frozen slopes, always following their guides: grooves, small lagoons of the most incredible blue color, gullies where water disappears into bottomless abysses are some of the experiences you will have during the two hour walk. A hike through the forest on your way back to the campsite and a picnic in front of the Glacier, complete your day while you await the boat that will take you back. The excursion lasts about 6 hours and costs u$s 60.

**Attention:** you have to take your own picnic basket.

### *Upsala and Spegazzini Glaciers and Onelli Bay*

This excursion, travels along the North Arm of Lake Argentino, one of the most beautiful areas of the National Park and only accessible by water. The trip is made on comfortable ships with bar, restrooms, audio, lounge and outdoor spaces. You embark at Punta Bandera, 45 km from Calafate and you sail for 2 and a half hours , among numerous icebergs, some of them several times the size of the ship, toward Upsala and Spegazzini Glaciers. Once you arrive before the Galciers, the ship stops and the ship guide explains  the surrounding landscape: glaciers and mountains form a touching setting that the visitor does not get tired of admiring. But the excursion is not over: you continue toward Bahía Onelli, where you debark to make a short walk within the forest, and at the end an unforgettable vision: The Onelli Bay, almost completely covered by icebergs, and where three glaciers (Agassiz, Bolados and Onelli) that come down from the frozen peaks of the Cordillera join.

Once on the ship again, you return to Punta bandera and from there by land to Calafate.

The excursion lasts about 10 hours and costs approximately u$s 79.- This price does not include land transportation Calafate-Punta Bandera-Calafate (u$s 20) and National Park entrance fee (u$s 5).

Lunch: There is a restaurant at Bahìa Onelli. Another possibility is to take your own snack and have it during the stop, which lasts about 3 and a half hours..

Other possible lake excursions in the zone:

### Upsala Glacier, Onelli Bay and walk to Heim Glacier

(Frequency every 3 days with 20 passengers minimum)

This tour has the same outline as the preceding excursion (except for Spegazzini Glacier), and allows you a walk in the forest up to the Heim Glacier Fall. It is commendable to people who enjoy hiking.. and to rise early, because the excursion leaves PUNTA BANDERA at 6,30 AM and returns to the port at 3,30 PM

*Price* u$s 40

### Cristina Channel

Inquiry on frequency in Calafate
Price: Between u$s 50 and 70

It is a privileged place within the cordillera, a former sheep estancia now transformed into a hotel. It is the starting point of many hikes such as Upsala Glacier, Patagonian Ice and the North Canyon. Ideal for ecotourism lovers who want to discover wild virgin places.

### Seno Mayo and Perito Moreno Glacier

(Frequency every 2 days with a minimum of 20 passengers)
You can enjoy the Seno Mayo, one of the most spectacular fiords of the zone , and the North front of the Perito Moreno Glacier from the water.
*Departure:* 12 PM. Returning to **Punta Bandera:** 7 PM
*Price:* u$s 30

### *Roca Lake*

The Roca Lake is located in the Southern area of Argentino Lake, and is connected to the latter by a narrow arm. It is famous for its abundant fishing of Rainbow and Canadien trout.

It is an ideal area for camping, with spectacular views of the Cordillera. The campsite has all facilities: restrooms, hot showers, cooking places, cafeteria-restaurant, lodging trailers, children's games, fishing gear rental..

There are many nice places in the surroundings for hiking in the forest or the lake coast,or to the repestrian paintings close by.

5 km to the West of the Roca Lake, stands Estancia Nibepo Aike, where there is a Country Hotel and a Tea Room.

There is also a free camping site with no facilities in the zone. We remind all the user to keep the place clean.5 km to the West of the Roca Lake, stands **Estancia Nibepo Aike**, where there is a country hotel and a Tea Room, worthwhile the visit.

### *Gualicho Caves - Rupestrian Caves*

Only 7 km from Calafate, first on the road to Río Gallegos and later on a gravel side road to the left, on the coast of Lake Argentino, there are some rocky formations, where the ancient indigenous populations left their mysterious prints in the form of rupestrian paintings.

Though the original paintings were quite deteriorated, on adjacent walls and using identical techniques and materials, the paintings have been reconstituted together with a selection of the main pictorial rupestrian manifestations of the Province of Santa Cruz.

There is a cafeteria with excellent panoramic views of the lake and the cordillera, as well as specialized guides on site.

### A one day outing on an Estancia

The Patagonian estancias to open their doors to tourism increase daily. A visit to one of them, is an ideal way to know about sheep raising and its protagonists. A horseback ride around the estancia, and later on, a real "asado al palo" (typical lamb barbecue), a gastronomic jewel of the region, will complete a perfect day.

Four estancias currently offer this one day outing to our visitors, at a short distance from Calafate:

**Estancia María Elisa / Franka**
40 km from Calafate on the road to Río Gallegos and another 10 km along the Río Bote Valley. Lodging. Horseback riding. It is run by its owners.

**Estancia Alice - El Galpón**
22 km from Calafate, on the road to Perito Moreno, by the Argentino Lake. Horseback riding. Bird watching. Demonstration of sheep shearing and work with sheep dogs. Restaurant.

**Estancia Huiliche**
Only 2 km from Calafate, on the road to Roca Lake. Panoramic views over Lago Argentino. Horse riding. Lodging.

**Estancia Nibepo Aike**
See Roca Lake.

## SERVICES IN EL CALAFATE
Telephone code:  From Argentina 02902
From foreign countries 542902
Postal code: 9405

### Hotels

| NAMES | ADDRESS | TELEPHONE |
|---|---|---|
| Posada Los Alamos | Gdor. Moyano 1355 | 491144 |
| Kautatún-Country Hotel | Estancia 25 de Mayo | 491059 |
| El Mirador del Lago | Avda Libertador 2047 | 491213 |
| Hostal del Cerro | Villa Parque Los Glaciares | 491310 |
| Michelangelo | Gob. Moyano | 491045 |
| Bahía Redonda | Calle 15 Nº 148 | 491314 |
| Kalkén | V. Feilberg 119 | 491073 |
| El Quijote | Gdor. Moyano 1191 | 491017 |
| Lar-Aike | Avda. del Libertador 2681 | 491306 |
| Kapenke | Gdor Gregores 1094 | 491093 |
| A.C.A. | 1 de Mayo 849 | 491004 |
| La Loma | J.A. Roca 849 | 491016 |
| Schilling | J.A. Roca 851 | 491453 |
| Paso Verlika | Avda. del Libertador 1108 | 491009 |
| Amado | Avda. del Libertador 1072 | 491023 |
| Upsala | Cmdte. Espora 139 | 491166 |

### Estancias - Inns

| | | | |
|---|---|---|---|
| Alta Vista | 30 km from Calafate | | 491247 |
| Nibepo-Aike | 48 km from Calafate | 02966 | 422262 |
| María Elisa | 45 km from Calafate | | |
| El Galpón | 22 km from Calafate | | 491793 |
| Los Notros | 5 km before Perito Moreno Clacier | | 491437 |

## Lodges

*Price:* Between u$s 10 y 15 p/pers.

| | | |
|---|---|---|
| Alejandra | Cmte. Espora 60 | 491328 |
| Amancay | Gdor Gregores 1457 | 491113 |
| El Arroyo | 25 de Mayo 343 | 491162 |
| Belén | Los Gauchos 300 | 491028 |
| Las Cabañitas | V. Feilberg 218 | 491118 |
| Del Norte | Los Gauchos 813 | 491117 |
| Jorgito | Gdor. Moyano 943 | 491323 |
| Lago Azul | Perito Moreno 83 | 491419 |
| Los Lagos | 25 de Mayo 220 | 491170 |
| Los Dos Pinos | 9 de Julio 358 | 491271 |
| Albergue de la Juventud | Los Pioneros n/n | 491243 |
| Albergue Lago Argentino | Campaña del Desierto 1050 | 491423 |

## Cabins

| | | |
|---|---|---|
| Nevis | Avda. del Libertador 1696 | 491180 |
| Isla Solitaria | Avda. del Libertador s/n | 491264 |
| Del Sol | Avda. del Libertador 1956 | 491439 |

## Campsites

Municipal - José Pantín s/n

## Restaurants

| | | |
|---|---|---|
| The Family House | Comandante Espora 18 | 491436 |
| Pizzería Onelli | Avda. del Libertador 1177 | 491184 |
| Pizzería El Rancho | Gdor. Moyano y 9 de Julio | 491644 |
| Pizzería Ref. Cerro Torre | Avda. del Libertador 990 | |
| La Esquina | Avda. del Libertador / 9 de Julio | 491709 |
| La Cocina | Avda. del Libertador 1245 | 491758 |

*Most of hotels offer restaurant service.*

## Restaurant - Folklore Show

Don Diego de la Noche        Avda. del Libertador 1603            491270

## Steak houses

La Tablita                   Cor. Rosales 24                      491065
Mi Viejo                     Avda. del Libertador 1132            491691

## Food to Take

La Moderna                   Avda. del Libertador 1132            491169

## Regional Products - Books - Maps -T Shirts

Planet Patagonia             Avda. del Libertador 958             492352
Open Calafate                Avda. del Libertador 996             491254
Creazzioni Donna             Avda. del Libertador 1180
La Leyenda                   Avda. del Libertador 1184            491364
Rincón Maipé                 Avda. del Libertador 1190
World's End                  Avda. del Libertador 1194
Michay                       C. Espora 48                         492347

## Homemade Chocolate

Casa Guerrero                Avda del Libertador 1249
Dulce Lugar                  Avda del Libertador/25 de Mayo

## Handicraft

Artenías Argentinas          Avda del Libertador 1215             491104
El Mercado Artesanal         Avda del Libertador 1208             491177
El Mercadito                 Avda del Libertador 1116             491640
La Casita                    Avda del Libertador

## Internet - E-mail

Cooperativa Telefónica       Comandante Espora 190

## HORSE RIDING

El Rancho                                                              491203

## BICYCLE RENTAL

Camping Municipal      José Pantín s/n

## MOTOR CUATRICYCLE RENTAL

Cuatri Rent            Avda del Libertador y C. Espora               491496

## CAR RENTAL

Freelander                                                             491437

## CASINO

Good Luck              1 de Mayo 50                                   491390

## CABARET

El Gran Judas          25 de Mayo y Gdor. Moyano

## PHOTOGRAPHY - DEVELOPING

Planet Patagonia       Avda. del Libertador 958                      492352
Open Calafate          Avda. del Libertador 996                      491254
Focus                  Avda. del Libertador 1124                     492210
Aonikenk               Avda del Libertador 1640                      491340

## PHARMACIES

Farmacia Minich        Avda del Libertador y C. Espora               492180
Farmacia Calafate      Avda del Libertador / 25 de Mayo

## LAUNDRIES

El Lavadero            Avda del Libertador 1118                      491264

**FOR FURTHER INFORMATION CONTACT THE LOCAL TOURISM BUREAU**

# EL CHALTEN

El Chalten, 220 km from Calafate, is an ideal place for mountain hiking lovers, trekking and several ecotourism activities: The beauty of the mountains and their easy access, have made this region an obligatory stop for any international tourism agency when programming an adventure trip.

Chaltén is the name the Tehuelches of the region called the peak that Perito Moreno would later baptize with the name of Fitz-Roy. In Aonikenk language it means "smoky mountain" The indians, as well as the first explorers of the area, including Perito Moreno, thought it was a volcano.

To avoid confusions, I have decided to call the town and the surroundings Chaltén (or El Chaltén) and the mountain Fitz-Roy.

The excursions that we briefly describe , can be done by any person in a normal physical condition. Of course, we suggest not to leave the demarcated trails and to keep the environment clean. Take a small bag to bring down the litter. For any information on the area, contact the local Tourism Bureau or Parkguards.

## BLANCO RIVER AND FITZ ROY BASE CAMP

*Duration*: 3 hours (one way)
*Level difference*: 300 m
*Maximum height*: 750 m.a.s.l. (Base Camp)
1160 m.a.s.l. (Laguna de los Tres)

1 km from town, the trail goes up through the lenga forests up to a panoramic view point (1 hour), from where you can see all Mount Fitz Roy and its surrounding needles. A little further on, (1 hr. 15 m), you find a deviation to the left that leads to **Laguna Capri** (5 min). Can Camp.

Following the trail , you arrive at **Poincenot Camp** (2hrs. 45 min. can Camp), and a little further on, after crossing **Blanco River**, you find Base Camp, where every year the mountain climbing expeditions stay while waiting for favorable weather conditions.

From there, along a quite steep slope, 1 hour ascension, you arrive at **Laguna de los Tres**, that has one of the most spectacular views of the Park.

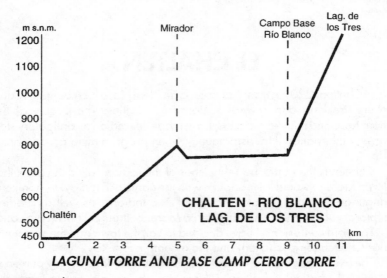

*LAGUNA TORRE AND BASE CAMP CERRO TORRE*

**Duration:** 3 hours
**Level diference:** 200 m.
**Maximum height:** 650 m.a.s.l.

The road starts off on a short and steepy slope, to later descend to the bed of the Fitz-Roy River Valley, getting closer and closer to the imposing Mount Torre and Mount de los Adela. After a two and a half hour walk, a sign suggests us two possibilities: to the left, **Bridwell Camp** (can camp) and the Torre Lagoon. To the right, **Maestri Camp** (camping forbidden) on the lateral moraine of the ancient Torre glacier. Any of these places has spectacular views of the neighboring mountains, standing out among them all the mythical **Mount Torre**.

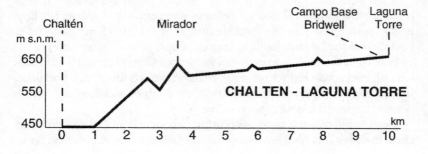

## PIEDRA DEL FRAILE

There are two ways to get to Piedra del Fraile:

From Blanco River, you go down along the left shore of the river course, and after crossing the Piedras Blancas stream, that leads to a glacier of the same name, you continue for 40 min longer, downward till you encounter the trail that borders the Eléctrico River up to Piedra del Fraile (2 more hours)

From the road to Lago del Desierto, 100 meters before crossing the bridge over Blanco river, there is a small trail that goes Westward, and that takes us in two hours up to Piedra del Fraile. From there, there are several possible hikes toward the base of the Aguja Guillaumet, Lago Eléctrico and Glaciar Marconi.

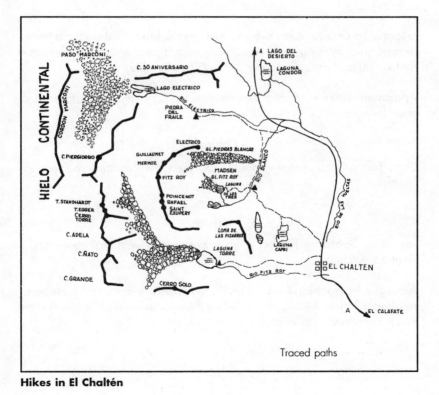

**Hikes in El Chaltén**

At Piedra del Fraile , there is a private campsite (**Refugio Los Troncos**) that has hot water, lodging, hot and cold drinks, a small restaurant...

## SERVICES IN EL CHALTEN

### Inns

**Fitz-Roy Inn:** Double rooms with private bathrooms. 2 double or quadruple room apartments with shared bathroom. Heating, Restaurant and breakfast room in the building.

**Lago del Desierto:** Double rooms with private bathroom. 6 bed rooms with shared bathroom. Heating. Restaurant and breakfast room in next door building.

**Estancia La Quinta:** 4 km before reaching the town. Old estancia transformed into lodging with quadruple rooms and shared bathrooms. Restaurant and breakfast room in next door building.

**Apartment-Hotel La Aldea**: Apartments for 5 people with kitchen and small livingroom.

### Cabins

**Cerro Torre:** Cabins with two double rooms each with bathroom. Heating. Fireplace.

### Lodging

**Los Ñires Boarding House:** 6 bunk-bed rooms with bathroom each. Heating. Kitchen.

**Albergue Patagonia:** 4 and 6 bunk bed rooms with shared bathroom. Heating. Kitchen. Restaurant. Excellent panoramic view of De Las Vueltas River. Warm atmosphere.

## RESTAURANTS
The Wall
La Senyera

## HOMEMADE CHOCOLATE
Josh Aike

## HANDCRAFTS - T SHIRTS - POSTCARDS
El Mercado Artesanal

## CAMPING, MOUNTAIN GEAR RENTAL
El Mercado Artesanal

## GROCERY STORES
There are three general goods stores in town.

## CAMP SITES:
There are two free camping sites near town and two private ones on the
road to Lago del Desierto. Estancia Ricanor, 20 km away and Camping
Lago del Desierto,  37 km on the south margin of the Lake, at the end of
the road.

## TELEPHONE
National and international telephone at Restaurant La Senyera

## HEALTH ASSISTANCE
Doctor, nurse, ambulances

## OTHER SERVICES
Trekking and Mountain Guides
Horseback Rides

## TREKKING MAPS

Monte Fitz Roy / Cerro Torre / Lago del Desierto, 1:50000,
Zagier & Urruty Publications.

**FOR FURTHER INFORMATION, CONTACT THE LOCAL TOURISM BUREAU**

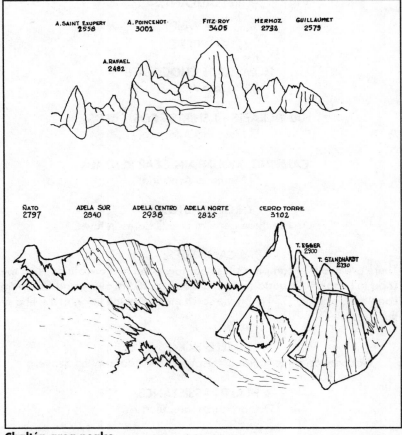

**Chaltén area peaks**